OF MEN, AND NOT OF LAW

In the government of this Commonwealth, the legislative department shall never exercise the executive and judicial powers, or either of them; the executive shall never exercise the legislative or judicial powers, or either of them; the judicial shall never exercise the legislative and executive powers, or either of them; to the end that it may be government of laws and not of men.

Constitution of the
Commonwealth of
Massachusetts
1780 A.D.

FOREWORD By

FRANK E. HOLMAN

Former President, American Bar Association

LYMAN A. GARBER

OF MEN AND NOT OF LAW

HOW THE COURTS ARE USURPING THE POLITICAL FUNCTION

THE DEVIN-ADAIR COMPANY

NEW YORK

218167

DEDICATION

To my confreres, both the living and the legions gone before, who have found much of the purpose of their lives in labor with the law.

FOREWORD

Mr. Lyman A. Garber, in his new book *Of Men, and Not of Law* has written a very timely expose of the flagrant usurpation of power by the Appellate Courts of the United States—both State and Federal. The author has avoided petty or captious criticism. He has kept accurate, both as to the law and the facts, and objective and constructive in his criticisms.

The book is well documented and proves that the Appellate Courts, in their decisions in recent years, by self-conceived judicial legislation (acting upon their views as men and not as interpreters of the law), have not only undermined and emasculated the Constitution of the United States but the Constitutions of various of the states. Their decisions are even shown to have led to an increase of crime by freeing hardened and convicted criminals on some mere technicality of procedure.

Every American lawyer and every layman interested in good government should read this book. It is entirely readable, even by laymen. I recommend it as one of the most revealing exposes of judicial usurpation yet produced.

Frank E. Holman

Seattle, Washington

ACKNOWLEDGMENT

I am deeply indebted to a number of friends for editorial assistance. My renewed expressions of appreciation go to Dr. Harry Elmer Barnes, historian and penologist; to Howard Heyn of the Associated Press; to my uncle, Vance Armentrout, editorial writer of the *Louisville Courior-Journal* and the *Louisville Times*; to Dr. Paul H. Sheats, Director of University Extension of the University of California; to businessmen Ralph Hilton and Vernon MacDonald Barton; to lawyers Karl F. Geiser, Stanley N. Gleis, Rodd Kelsey, and Robert J. Kelleher, Captain of the Davis Cup team that brought the Davis Cup back to America in 1963; and, to the nth degree, to my wife who, as Marian Carter, in her ten years as Program Director of America's Town Meeting of the Air, developed an uncompromising editorial eye. I trust that the labors of these people may be, at least in a reasonable degree, justified in this book.

contents

OF MEN, AND NOT OF LAW

one

Which Comes First, the Government Or the Law?

So far as recorded history discloses (over 5000 years) no finer form of government than the American system has been devised by man. Measured by degree of personal liberty and individual freedom from the dictates of arbitrary power, the American Federal Republic is the world's most truly revolutionary concept of government. And it has worked.

Despite the success it has scored, the American system has been, and now is, under serious attack by Americans. Already many of its basic principles have been altered or emasculated. In military parlance, our federal constitutional republic has been put on the defensive, and its main line of resistance has been breached at many places. Ever mounting in intensity, the offensive is a continuing one. Surprisingly, even members of groups steeped in the traditions of American government, who might logically have been counted upon as last-ditch fighters in defense of the American system, have been indifferent, or passive, or even joined the ranks of the attackers.

This is notably true of the legal fraternity where unanimous loyalty to established principles and vast strength for the defense might have been anticipated. But unanimous support has not materialized. While a great fraction of the Nation's lawyers and judges adhere to traditional principles, many lawyers and judges are in the attackers' ranks—though the thrust of the attack is toward the eventual destruction of this nation; a nation conceived as one of law, not of men.

Law, in the United States, touches so many activities that it appears to be the governing power of the nation, however the axiom *the whole is greater than any of its parts* shows that this cannot be. Law's more restricted role is at once perceived in a simpler form of government, such as a dictatorship or an absolute monarchy. In such governments some trace of law is always present, but in degree it may vary from the level of mere "standard operating procedure" to something as pervasive as Bonaparte's all-comprehending Code Napoleon. Law obviously is a tool of the power that governs.

The most specific term for the power to govern is sovereignty, but with its suggestion of royalty, sovereignty seems incongruous when applied to a Swiss Republic on the one hand, or to a Stalin or a Hitler on the other.

Nevertheless, every government during its period of existence is sovereign. As we all know, the thirteen former British colonies were all sovereign nations at the time they entered into the contract we know as the Constitution of the United States of America. The colonies strove during Revolutionary days; strove in the post-Revolutionary days; and ultimately—through the text of the Constitution of the United States of America—strove to establish this "government of law, not of men." They succeeded to a substantial degree in their effort. That they succeeded at all is due to two main factors: first, they drafted wisely; second, the men, who were given positions of power, heeded, or were forced to heed, the limitations put on their powers by the constitutions of the several states and of the nation.[1]

In recent years, we have seen in the United States a great drifting away from strict adherence to the limitations of constitutions and of traditional law. And in this trend the legal fraternity plays a role that can be confus-

---

[1] In the recent past the American system commanded the almost unanimous support of lawyers and judges. The following excerpt from the inaugural speech of American Bar Association president, Frank E. Holman, was printed on the front cover of the Association's Journal of October, 1948. At that time it probably reflected the thinking of the overwhelming majority of the membership. "We of this profession are sworn to uphold the institutions and liberties which have made our nation great and our people free. We are pledged to a federal republic, to the constitutional separation of the powers of government, to the rights and duties of States and localities, to resistance to encroachments by any one department of government upon any other, to the defense of individual rights against arbitrary powers and against bureaucratic centralizations which break down the impartial rule of law and substitute uncontrolled official discretions."

ing to laymen. Since lawyers and judges deal largely in rules promulgated by government, laymen tend to think of them as experts on every aspect of government, even "why" a government happens to exist. But the fact is that on basic matters of government—how one is created, or is destroyed—the training of attorneys does not render them even knowledgeable as compared with such practical students of sovereignty as Washington, Napoleon, Bolivar, Juarez, Batista, Nasser, Castro, Trujillo, Diem, Kerensky, Hitler, Lenin—each of whom worked with the raw forces that create a sovereign, or destroy a sovereign.

Obviously the lawyer's professional point of view is not the same, for the very concept of law presupposes a government that exists and one that will continue to exist. It follows naturally that neither the teaching in law schools nor the normal practice of law is concerned with the health of the sovereign. The lawyer, nevertheless, like every other citizen, should be aware that governments are mortal for the fact is disclosed in the long obituary columns of history. The United States, we all know, will not endure forever, but we hope it will long endure.

Although every American should be deeply concerned for the health of the nation, many, including many lawyers and judges, with apparent *unconcern,* are sponsors of trends that must endanger it. Since the examples of such actions touch on elementary principles of sovereignty and law, let us briefly consider basic principles.

As is known to people of every continent, life is made pleasanter by gadgets, services, and conveniences. But in any survival sense even the humblest of these is a luxury. The basic requirements for human existence are simple: food, clothing, and shelter.

The basic requirement of government, too, is simple. A government exists while some individual or organization is able to enforce its will over a given people in a given area. All writers[2] on jurisprudence have touched on this subject. Blackstone said, "There is and must be in all (governments) a supreme, irresistible, absolute, uncontrolled authority, in which the *jura sumni imperii* or the rights of sovereignty reside."[3]

Ever paralleling sovereignty is a question: What conditions will keep the sovereign alive? Sure answers to that question are not readily apparent.

Elements of magnificence, beauty, tradition, humanity, science, reason, justice, or culture that may flourish under a government do not guarantee its survival. Neither the art of Greece, nor its exaltation of reason sufficed. Massive masonry, engineered roads, and codified law did not sustain the Roman sovereignty.

Culture, ubiquitous in France, has been an ineffectual bystander during a procession of governments from the monarchy of Louis XVI, First Republic, Directory, Consulate, Empire of Napoleon I, Bourbon Restoration of Louis XVIII, Bourgeois Kingdom of Louis Phillipe, Second Republic of Louis Napoleon Bonaparte, Empire of Louis Napoleon, Third Republic, Government of Vichy, Fourth Republic, to de Gaulle's Fifth Republic.

Judges and lawyers may be cultural embellishments, but they are not essentials of sovereignty. Governments can exist without trial by jury; most do. The greater part of the world's population throughout recorded time and

---

[2] Jurisprudence, Pound, 316
Lectures on Jurisprudence, Austin 5 Ed (1885) 295
[3] Commentaries, Blackstone (1765) 49

the larger portion of the world's land areas have been ruled by governments under which "law," by Anglo-Saxon standards, simply did not exist.

But history teaches this: No government has existed except where an individual or an organization has had the physical power to enforce the governing will.

There is little excuse for any literate American to forget that a fair degree of law and order is achievable only when police power is so overwhelming that none but psychopathic persons dare break the law.[4] Consider the events that followed the strike of the Boston Police in 1919. When the Police went off duty, lawless mobs took to the streets. Pillage and sacking were rampant until Governor Calvin Coolidge sent in the National Guard. A vast potential for violence had been seething, beneath the surface, even in staid old Boston!

Law and order prevail only so long as there is a "lid" to suppress disorder. This lid is the sovereign's control of overwhelming physical force. If the lid is removed, the reaction is explosive.

Just like every government that ever existed, our government is based primarily on physical force—though many present day lawyers, and judges, and legally educated statesmen seem to have lost sight of this simple fact. And apparently lulled by the gargantuan size of the United States, these practitioners prescribe very strong political drugs and nostrums for this country; prescribe **without** concern for the size of the dose, or for the potency of the drug.

————

[4] Reference here is not to the occasional regulation that is widely flouted, such as the Volstead Act.

One such prescription, a movement called World Peace Through Law that is based upon an intriguing half-truth, has become a principal activity of Bar Associations within the past ten years. It has attracted numerous lawyers as workers and commanded impressive financial support. With deference to the fine lawyers who are its proponents —in full sympathy with their justifiable pride in their profession—with complete recognition of the unselfish humanitarian motives behind their efforts—this question is raised: Does the movement for World Peace Through Law serve the fundamental interest of the United States? It is suggested here that it does not.

The title, "World Peace Through Law," is incomplete and dangerously misleading. The name conveys the thought that law has some self-enforcing quality. This is not so. No such thing as "law" exists unless there is the combination of a court, plus adequate force. Without the combination of a court and physical power there can be diplomacy, cooperation, arbitration, capitulation, negotiation, intimidation, or any form of acquiescence—but not law.[5]

---

[5] "There can be no effective law in the affairs of men or nations without an effective government having the following powers: The power to establish law (legislative); the power to authoritatively interpret law (judicial); and the power to effectively enforce law (executive). These three powers are the sine qua non of a rule of law. Without them there can no more be a rule of law than there can be a molecule of water without two atoms of hydrogen and one of oxygen. In some forms of government, these powers have been merged—in monarchies or absolute governments the three sometimes in the persons of the ruler with or without the aid of councilors; in others they have been only partially merged; and in a few, such as our own, there is a separation of these three basic powers. Nevertheless, in every instance of effec-

The name of the movement should be amplified to World Peace Through a *Constabulary* and Law, or to World Peace Through Law and *a Sheriff's Posse*. For the brief name, "World Peace Through Law," suggesting that citizens obey the law because it is written in books or spoken by judges, states a hazardous half-truth. The truth-half is that there are many citizens who voluntarily perform their contracts, behave equitably, and refrain from criminal acts. The other half is that a great mass of citizens conform to such standards, but only in acquiescence to overwhelming force.

Of course the proponents of World Peace Through Law may be convinced that sovereigns, unlike individuals, would all accede to judicial decree unsupported by force. Speculation on this could be interesting. How would Ghengis Khan, Napoleon, Hitler, Mussolini, or Stalin have reacted to such a notion?

Let us imagine the ghosts of these five historical figures were asked this question: "Assuming that a well spelled-out system of international law had existed during your rule, would it have deterred you from your conquests?" We may imagine their replies, somewhat as follows:

Ghengis: No. There was no one to enforce any law.

Napoleon: Ridiculous! Such law would not have been consistent with my manifest destiny.

---

tive human government there must exist all three—a legislative, a judicial and an executive authority—which, if we are to have world law, necessarily adds up to World Government." (Frank E. Holman, former President of the American Bar Association; Pamphlet entitled "The Problems of the World Court and the Connally Reservation"; Frayn Printing Company, Seattle; July 25, 1960).

Hitler: There was supposed to be such law, and a
            League of Nations to administer it. Then
            Litvinov duped the League into a program
            of Collective Security to support expansion
            of Communist Popular Fronts. Was that
            what you call 'law'?

Mussolini: Have you forgotten that the League of Na-
            tions said that my invasion of Ethiopia was
            against the law?

Stalin: Law is for the Capitalist fools. We Socialists
            are above law. We follow whatever course
            will advance world Socialism.

Are lawyers, in espousing World Peace Through Law,
overlooking the true nature of law and order?

It may be assumed that sophisticated systems of local
law—if supported by efficient police departments—could
improve in many nations the quotient of law, and order,
and justice. But that is a *domestic* problem. When we turn
to the problem of *World* Peace Through Law, it is immediately apparent that the utterly insurmountable problem
is how to enforce a judgment of a court? Today the military potentials of the U.S.A. and the U.S.S.R. simply
dwarf that of all other nations combined. Without the
acquiescence of both of these nations it would be impossible to assemble an international *force* to back a
court's decree.

For emphasis on this point, look at the changes wrought
during recent history. A tenable argument for World
Peace Through Law could well have been advanced after
World War I. As the world then existed, it would have

been feasible—on paper at least—to assemble a military force that would have been adequate against any one nation on earth except, possibly, the United States.

At that time France had by far the most powerful land force in the world. Great Britain had only one peer as a naval power, and the Empire gave her unparalleled aspects of strength. Italy achieved for a time a formidable air power. Germany had potential strength. Russia was a Second-Class power but with a great manpower reserve. Japan was strong on land and sea. The United States Navy was a force in readiness; America had proved its ability to mobilize a great army. Many Third-Class powers could then offer substantial military assistance.

No similar picture can be drawn now. Russia has bulged westward swallowing Lithuania, Latvia, Esthonia, and strategic parts of Finland. Through the amazing apparatus of the Communist Party, it dominates Poland, East Germany, Czechoslovakia, Rumania, Bulgaria, Hungary, Jugoslavia, and Albania. It has an arsenal of terrifying modern weapons and a formidable fleet of submarines. In fact, the U.S.S.R. and the U.S.A. are the only Great Powers in the world, and they present such wide margins of strength over all others that it might be said there are no nations in the *classic category* of Second-Class powers. Even the Third-Class ranks are thinned.

How can a decisive military force be raised among the nations of the world today to back a court's decree?

The extreme imbalance of power, existing since the end of World War II, was glaringly apparent in what President Truman characterized a "police action"—the 1950-1953 Korean activity. Because the troops of several nations took part in throwing up that roadblock to Communist expansion, the army of the United Nations might be thought of as a sheriff's posse. But such a concept suffers because of one stark fact. No effective posse in Korea could have been formed unless it had the United States of America as one of the deputies. And what kind of policing force is it that can come into being only if one particular citizen, in this case, Uncle Sam, joins up?

Or let us twirl the globe half around and look at the Congo. Possibly the United Nations' forces that left it in 1964, panting and exhausted, would be held by some observers to have performed adequately a peace-keeping assignment. But "The Law" could not be counted on to bring peace all over the world with a military force only effective against scattered Congolese tribesmen; "The Law" would need to be coupled with power great enough to confront an aggressor backed by the full might of Red China and the U.S.S.R.

Does any proponent of World Peace Through Law contend, even dream, that naked "law" could have "enjoined" the Chinese operation that engulfed North Viet Nam? "Enjoined" the Chinese conquest of Tibet?

Some proponents might object that the dead past does not fairly weigh World Peace Through Law, since this reform looks toward the future, and that future is assumed to be illumined by mutual understanding. Let us test such a theory on some presently visible situations.

Consider the problem of Israel. Would the proponents of World Peace Through Law suggest that a court, ruling on the ownership of the land now occupied by Israel, could render a decision that would be accepted either by the Israelis or the Arabs *if the losing party believed it had the physical power to resist the decision?*

Or consider the tragedy of the armed conflict that broke out in September, 1965, between India and Pakistan. Such events always wring from thoughtful men the anguished cry, "There must be a better way!" Would the proponents of World Peace Through Law suggest their formula is that better way? Would the proponents suggest that the "judgment" of a court could have detached Kashmir, which is overwhelmingly Moslem, from Hindu India, and delivered it to the "rightful" control of Moslem Pakistan? Or could the "judgment" of a court have quelled the Pakistini ambitions to control Kashmir?

Such questions are not the most difficult on our horizon; they do not directly involve the Communist drive for world empire. But they do suggest a danger in the lawyer's program. If the main effect of propagandizing for World Peace Through Law should be to induce an unfounded complacency in the non-Communist world, it can only react to further the advance of Communist-Socialism—a cruel hoax on every free man and every free woman.

The lawyers advocating World Peace Through Law are prescribing a very potent drug.

An even more dangerous prescription is the recommendation of many lawyers—voting as Members of the House of Delegates of the American Bar Association—to repeal the Connally Amendment.

As many lawyers can recall, the Permanent Court of International Justice, established in 1921, was superseded in 1946 by the International Court of Justice, commonly referred to as the "World Court." The World Court has no comprehensive statutes, no established guiding prin-

ciples. Thirty per cent of the bench of the 1946 Court
has been composed of biased judges (placed there by Communist countries).

Most of the nations that acknowledge the authority of
the World Court place reservations on its jurisdiction.
For example, the United States, by its Connally Amendment, denies the Court jurisdiction over internal affairs
of this nation. Further, it reserves to this nation the sole
right to determine what affairs *are* of domestic concern, as
opposed to those subject to international jurisdiction.

Prima facie this limitation on the World Court ex-
hibits—for us Americans in particular—the most elementary display of caution. Notwithstanding, the American
Bar Association, by majority votes of its House of Delegates in 1948 and 1960, counselled the Nation to repeal
the Connally Amendment. These recommendations are
clearly based on the same rationale as World Peace
Through Law.

The proponents of repeal relied upon restrictions of
the World Court's jurisdiction, but our own history has
demonstrated the elasticity of such limitations: The
United States Constitution granted to Congress jurisdiction over "navigable rivers." Americans have seen these
words, "navigable rivers," construed to justify Congress in
taxing North Dakota farmers to build flood control dams
on dry creeks rising in the mountains of Los Angeles
County, flowing through wealthy Los Angeles County,
and discharging into the Pacific Ocean in Los Angeles
County! They have seen Congressional jurisdiction over
"interstate commerce" expanded to embrace even the
wages of men who wash windows of buildings housing
businesses with interstate ramifications!

Further, the recent performances of other courts functioning on the international stage should not lead any observer to the sanguine expectation of high quality procedure or judgment from a World Court. War Crimes trials,[6] conducted by international tribunals for half a decade after the end of World War II, were variously authorized and constituted. The trials were carried on by eminent jurists and attorneys, and they proceeded with the tacit approval of most of the bench and bar of this and other nations. But these Allied trials in Italy, Germany, and Japan typically ignored basic tenets of law. They flouted The Hague Convention and The Geneva Convention. They created *ex post facto* crimes, they scarcely pretended to impartiality, and they acted—occasionally by preference—on inferior evidence. By executing and imprisoning military and naval officers of conquered nations the international courts reintroduced elements of warfare that had, in large measure, been abandoned for centuries by nations that professed to be civilized.

Whether the World Court will, or will not, model itself after the Allied War Crime Courts is a question for the lawyers who recommend that the United States submit to the unrestricted jurisdiction of the World Court. What do they predict?

In evaluating the Connally Amendment, many of the American Bar Association's proponents of repeal cast lawyerlike caution to the winds. They speak to the general effect that—if the United States were to set the example

---

[6] F. J. P. Veale estimates upwards of 24,000 War Crimes trials were held in the 18 months following the close of hostilities in World War II. Veale; *Advance to Barbarism;* C. C. Nelson Co., Appleton, Wis; page 202; 1953.

by exposing itself to the jurisdiction of a loosely defined World Court—previously selfish sovereignties, now regenerate, would crowd the aisles of the tabernacle.

As a notable example of reckless counselling, proponents of repeal of the Connally Amendment have offered many predictions that the World Court would display judicial self-restraint. Of necessity these were mainly speculative reassurances, but scarcely justifiable ones from American lawyers who have been close observers of the lack of self-restraint in our own courts—courts which are heir to one of the finest judicial traditions of all history.

This great sovereignty could be well served by public-minded lawyers who would apply to the affairs of the United States the same jealous caution and concern they automatically apply to the affairs of their individual clients. But advocating unqualified acceptance of World Court jurisdiction simply does not conform to any reasonable standard of caution.

Let us examine the record to see if our United States courts and state courts have exercised the kind of self-restraint that would forecast protection of the United States in the international forum.

two

Invasions of Sovereignty

Much of the vocal leadership in the trend to whittle away the sovereignty of the United States has come from lawyers acting in the capacity of volunteers.

However, actual invasions of sovereignty, covering most of the legal spectrum, have been effected by judicial decisions progressively curtailing vital freedom of action of the state and national governments. The lack of self-restraint by our Appellate Courts is the most dramatic judicial manifestation of our times. The broad sweep of this movement is only suggested by examples drawn from five widely divergent areas of the law:

1. Executive responsibility
2. Sovereign immunity

3. Law of evidence
4. Ignorance of the law
5. Double jeopardy

The examples disclose high court judges—vested with power, but self-freed of restraint—releasing an ever swelling flood of decisions that undermine the foundations on which this Nation was built.

They also disclose many high court justices who stand on the Constitutional bases of their courts' power, and whose earnest words in dissenting opinions bespeak their disquietude over judicial outreachings.

1. EXECUTIVE RESPONSIBILITY: From statistics on the millions of persons employed by the executive branches of the national, state, and local governments, it may be seen that employing faithful and competent persons is a responsibility of great magnitude. In recent years, however, the prerogative of the executive to hire and fire has been greatly circumscribed by the judiciary. The following example discloses the Supreme Court of the United States substituting its judgment for the judgment of the executive.[1]

A Professor Slochower of Brooklyn College had been subpoenaed to testify before a Congressional committee. He had refused to answer questions of the committee about his possible Communist affiliations, pleading the Fifth Amendment exemption against self-incrimination. As a consequence the Board of Higher Education of the City of New York dismissed him. When he sued for re-instatement the New York courts upheld the Board. Pro-

---

[1] *Slochower v. Board of Higher Education of City of New York,* 350 U S 551 (1956)

fessor Slochower then petitioned the United States Supreme Court. There a majority of the justices—overriding the professor's own assertion that his answer as to Communist activities would tend to incriminate him—ruled that he should be reinstated as a teacher! And recover back pay amounting to approximately $40,000.00.

In a noteworthy dissent, joined by Justices Burton and Minton, Justice Reed said the Fifth Amendment might serve to keep a citizen out of jail, but not to qualify him for a professorship!

> . . . such avoidance of public duty to furnish information can properly be considered to stamp the employee as a person unfit to hold certain official positions . . . The fact that the witness had a right to plead the privilege against self-incrimination protects him against prosecution but not against the loss of his job. . . The city does have reasonable grounds to require its employees either to give evidence regarding facts of official conduct within their knowledge or to give up the positions they hold . . . Those charged with educational duties in a State bear heavy responsibilities . . . A teacher works in a sensitive area in a school room. There he shapes the attitude of young minds towards the society in which they live . . . That the school authorities have the right and duty to screen the officials, teachers, and employees as to their fitness to maintain the integrity of the schools as part of ordered society, cannot be doubted.

The heart of the issue was that the decision on employing Professor Slochower was a function of the executive. In substituting a court's appraisal for the Board's appraisal of the professor's qualifications, the judiciary was *violating a basic tenet of our tripartite form of government.*

2. SOVEREIGN IMMUNITY: The doctrine that a sovereign may not be sued, except with the sovereign's express consent, was part of English law at the time of our Revolution.[2] Whatever the origin of the doctrine of sovereign immunity may have been, the rule of law has a very practical basis: If a government's treasury were emptied to satisfy judgments, the government could no longer function.

Every government is limited in the amount it can spend by its available income, and the credit that will be extended to it. The limits to spending are facts, not abstractions. Some citizens are too young to remember the plight of the multitude of bankrupt towns and counties in the 1930's; to remember that, just before Fiorello La Guardia became mayor of New York in 1933, a "revolving loan" to the City of New York was being passed—like a hot potato—from one of Manhattan's banks to the next.

Overextension is not merely a depression happening. At any given moment, many governmental units throughout the nation are in financial trouble. In very recent years, the State of Michigan went through a money crisis. Currently, repatriating dependents of foreign-based soldiers, sailors, and marines is an intimate reminder that gold in the vaults of Fort Knox is at a dangerously low level. The financial problem is universal and ever-present; there is no legislative body that is not harrassed by the need to provide money for existing and desired undertakings, and by the necessity of rejecting projects that can not be paid for.

Those examples of financial problems are drawn from

---

[2] *Russell v. Men of Devon*, 100 Eng Rep. 359.

modern times, but governmental solvency has been a matter of concern for generations. Undoubtedly recognition of the importance of solvency led to the ready and early acceptance of the English doctrine of sovereign immunity[3] by our state and federal courts. In 1862, only a dozen years after admission of the State of California into the Union, it was established in California that a government-supported hospital (since it was a part of the sovereign) would not be liable for the negligent acts of its officers or employees.[4] Ninety-nine years later in a decision remarkable for its frank disregard of the existing law, and of the constitutional limits of judicial authority, the California Supreme Court struck down the doctrine.

It did so in a situation that focuses on the ever-present problem of trying to meet civic needs with available finances and discloses the vital role of sovereign immunity in protecting government activities against possibly ruinous judgments for damages.[5] The citizens of a sparsely populated area in Tehama County, California, around the town of Corning, population 3,000, feeling the need for local hospital facilities, had formed a governmental hos-

-----

[3] The immunity of the sovereign is not a blanket exemption from liability. Broadly speaking the rule has been that governments are liable for damages they inflict in their "ministerial" capacities; are not liable for damages they inflict in their "governmental" capacities (war, fire, police, etcetera). From time to time, on both state and national levels, the application of the doctrine of sovereign immunity has—with complete propriety—been modified by legislatures. Changing existing rules of law is a prerogative of a legislature. It is not a prerogative of the judiciary.

[4] *Sherbourne v. Yuba County,* 21 Cal 113 (1862)

[5] *Muskoff v. Corning Hospital District,* 55 Cal 2d 211 (1961)

pital district that supported the Corning Memorial Hospital.

Obviously such a hospital district, supported by a small population, could not have inexhaustible financial resources; conceivably it could be forced to close Memorial Hospital if acts of negligence by employees occurred and resulted in large judgments for damages. In due course the Corning Memorial Hospital had as one of its patients a Mrs. Muskoff. While she was a patient she was allegedly injured through the negligence of the hospital staff, and brought suit against the hospital. The trial court dismissed her suit on the ground of sovereign immunity. In reversing the trial court's judgment—and establishing a new rule of law—The California Supreme Court candidly stated:

> After a re-evaluation of the rule of governmental immunity from . . . liability we have concluded that it must be discarded as mistaken and unjust.*

The *unconstitutionality* of such legislating by the high Court was pointed to by Justice Schauer in a dissenting opinion in which he was joined by Justice McComb:

> As recently as 1958 this court . . . held that 'abrogation or restriction of this doctrine (governmental immunity) is primarily a legislative matter' . . . But today's majority . . . usurp the legislative function . . .

---

* *Author's Note:* Judges who have been concerned with a matter at issue obviously speak with great authority. Quotations from their opinions are used here and at many places throughout the book. It is a matter of regret that the limits of space dictate that in general only the briefest excerpts from the courts' opinions can be presented. Although in many places quotations are from dissenting opinions, it may be worthy of special notice that much of the available space has been allotted to opinions of the majority.

Our state Constitution provides, 'The powers of the government of the State of California shall be divided into three separate departments—the legislative, executive, and judicial; and no person charged with the exercise of powers properly belonging to one of these departments shall exercise any functions appertaining to either of the others, except as in this Constitution expressly directed or permitted' . . .

3. THE LAW OF EVIDENCE: Two relatively recent forces in America—the flood-tide of criminal activity and Communist infiltration—seem to have stimulated, perversely enough, new judicial rules that set up road blocks for police and prosecutors. The broadest sweep of this restrictive judicial legislating has been in the field of evidence. How the repression of crime and subversion is being rendered increasingly difficult is suggested by three cases, each of which created a new and restrictive rule of evidence.

The federal courts for many years have been excluding valid evidence of crime—if it was obtained by "unlawful" means (the exclusionary evidence rule). The exclusionary evidence rule works this way: If a police officer discovers evidence of a crime, but a judge later decides he had no right to be searching where he saw or heard the evidence, the evidence is scrapped.

This scrapping of proof of guilt, often conclusive proof, is coin of infinitely great value to the criminal. Of this there is no question. There is a question, however, whether such an artificial defense is of any value to society, or is called for under the Constitution; in fact there are observers who indict the exclusionary evidence rule as a brutal, conscienceless device, inflicting needless loss of life, limb, and property on law-abiding citizens. Nevertheless it is extolled by some judges and some lawyers.

Decision by decision and at an increasing tempo during recent years, the federal courts have widened such grounds for suppressing evidence; more and more criminals whose unquestionable guilt was shown on trial, or could have been shown, have been freed to prey upon society again. It is to be noted that the exclusionary evidence rule has historically been rejected in the state courts—where the overwhelming preponderance of criminal prosecutions are handled. However, the new fashions in law-making have begun to lead state courts, too, to overrule their long established principles for admitting evidence.

California's Cahan decision[6] is a case in point. In this now-famous decision the California Supreme Court legislated a sweeping change in the state's law of evidence and freed a racketeer whose guilt was clearly established through evidence obtained by hidden microphones.

The following excerpts from the decision disclose the facts of the case:

> Defendant and 15 other persons were charged with conspiring to engage in horse-race-bookmaking and related offenses in violation of section 337a of the Penal Code . . . Charles H. Cahan, one of the defendants found guilty . . . appeals . . . Gerald Wooters, an officer attached to the intelligence unit of that department testified that after securing the permission of the chief of police . . . (he made) microphone installations at two places occupied by defendants . . .

In rejecting such undebatable evidence of the defendant's guilt, the court offered this justification:

---

[6] *People of the State of California v. Cahan,* 44 Cal 2d 434 (1954)

. . . it bears emphasis that the court is not concerned solely with the rights of the defendant before it, however guilty he may appear, *but with the constitutional rights of all of the people to be secure in their homes, persons, and effects* . . . (italics added)

The court's reasoning suggests a searching question: Would the average law-abiding citizen choose *to be secure in his home, person, and effects* against (1) zealous police officers, or (2) murderers, rapists, burglars, robbers, and other criminals who, but for the exclusionary evidence rule, might be safely lodged in prison?

The strongly worded dissent of Justice Spence was joined by Justices Shenk and Edwards:

The guilt of the appellant is clearly demonstrated by the record before us. He and his numerous co-defendants unquestionably engaged in a far-reaching conspiracy to commit innumerable violations of the laws of the State of California. Six of his co-defendants pleaded guilty and seven others, in addition to appellant, were convicted upon the trial. We have before us solely the appeal of defendant Charles H. Cahan. Upon the trial, certain evidence was admitted over the objection that it had been illegally obtained. The trial judge, following precisely the non-exclusionary rule which . . . had been firmly established as the law of this state, admitted the evidence . . . The spectacle of an obviously guilty defendant . . . obtaining immunity from any successful prosecution . . . is a picture which has been too often seen in the federal practice. In speaking of an obviously guilty defendant, I refer by way of example to one from whose home has been taken large quantities of contraband, consisting of narcotics. . . It must be remembered that petitioner is not invoking the Constitution . . . to recover reparations for the violation. . . That the rule of exclusion . . .

results in the escape of guilty persons is more capable of demonstration than that it deters invasions of rights by the police . . . Thus, it appears that the main beneficiaries of the adoption of the exclusionary rule will be those members of the underworld who prey upon law-abiding citizens through their criminal activities . . . the cost of the adoption of the exclusionary rule is manifestly too great . . .

There was an ironic aftermath of the decision. Mr. Cahan was murdered.

The exclusionary rule has since been arbitrarily imposed upon every state in the Union. On its last decision day for the term ending June 1961, the United States Supreme Court stated a new rule of law:

We hold that all evidence obtained by searches and seizure in violation of the Constitution is . . . inadmissible in a state court.[7]

Another evidence decision occasioned an unusual amount of comment when it was announced, and the comment was unusually critical.

The case was *Jencks v. United States.*[8] The defendant, Jencks, was president of a local of International Mine, Mill and Smelter Workers. He was tried on two counts of falsely swearing that he was not a member of, or affiliated with, the Communist Party. Two F.B.I. agents, who had been accepted into the Communist Party, were principal witnesses for the prosecution. At the trial the defendant sought to have the agents' reports to the F.B.I. examined by the trial judge, and to have the judge allow the de-

---

[7] *Mapp v. Ohio,* 364 US 868 (1961)
[8] *Jencks v. United States,* 353 US 657 (1957)

fendant access to those portions that the trial judge might consider valuable as evidence. The request was denied. Jencks was convicted.

On appeal the Supreme Court made a sweeping ruling on the law of evidence:

> We now hold that the petitioner was entitled to an order directing the Government to produce for inspection *all* reports (of the F.B.I. agents) in its possession, written and, when orally made, as recorded by the F.B.I., touching the events and activities as to which they testified at the trial. We hold, further, that the petitioner is entitled to inspect the reports to decide whether to use them in his defense.

In his dissent Justice Clark expressed his alarm at this new rule of evidence:

> Even the defense attorneys did not have the temerity to ask for such a sweeping decision. They only asked that the documents be delivered to the judge for his determination of whether the defendant should be permitted to examine them . . . The rule announced today has no support in any of our cases. Every federal judge and every lawyer of federal experience knows that it is not the present rule. Director J. Edgar Hoover back in 1950 tellingly pointed this out before a Subcommittee of the Committee on Foreign Relations of the United States Senate: . . . 'I have always maintained the view that if we were to fully discharge the serious responsibilities imposed upon us, the confidential character of our files must be inviolate . . . If spread upon the record, criminals, foreign agents, subversives, and others would be forewarned and would seek methods to carry out their activities by avoiding detection and thus defeat the very purpose for which the F.B.I. was created'.

The breakneck pace of legislating-via-court-decisions

was spotlighted on December 16, 1957. On that day the Supreme Court announced two precedent-breaking decisions. These are discussed under topics 4 and 5.

4. IGNORANCE OF THE LAW: Up to December 16, 1957, laymen were correct in their understanding of one legal principle—that ignorance of the law is no excuse. But by the decision of *Lambert v. The People of the State of California,*[9] even this North Star has been removed from the legal firmament. The amazing new ruling came on a petition to the United States Supreme Court by a previously convicted forger who had failed to register as such under the Municipal Code of Los Angeles. The defendant pleaded ignorance of the law—that she did not know she was supposed to register.

Justice Frankfurter said that if such a defense were to become established law it would require a large book merely to list the national, state, city, town, and county statutes and ordinances that would be unenforceable. But the prospect of so impeding the enforcement of many laws did not deter the majority of the Supreme Court who ruled:

> Where a person did not know of the duty to register and where there was no proof or probability of such knowledge, he may not be convicted consistently with due process.

Justice Frankfurter, dissenting with Justices Harlan and Whittaker, offered this pious hope in closing his opinion:

> I feel confident that the present decision will turn out to be an isolated deviation—a derelict on the waters of the law.

---

[9] *Lambert v. People of the State of California,* 355 US 255 (1957)

5. DOUBLE JEOPARDY: The Constitution of the United States and the constitutions of most or all of the states provide that a defendant shall not be twice put in jeopardy for the alleged commission of a crime. In the United States Constitution the wording is, "nor shall any person be subject for the same offense to be twice put in jeopardy of life or limb."

Clearly, if a jury brings in a not-guilty verdict, a person has been once in jeopardy and cannot be re-tried for the same offense. But what if the jury finds him guilty and he appeals and the conviction is set aside? Can he be tried again? In other words, is the whole proceeding—trial, reversal, re-trial—one jeopardy, or is the re-trial a second jeopardy? Since early days the rule in Federal Courts has been that it is all part of the same jeopardy—the defendant can be tried again.

A related question arises in a situation such as this: A defendant is charged with both first and second degree murder; he is convicted of *second* degree murder; he appeals and wins a new trial. Can the jury in the new trial find him guilty of the greater offense; of first degree murder? For over a century the answer in the federal courts was "Yes."

In portentous words, spoken October 13, 1846, Justice Grier expounded the working of this rule. Three defendants had been jointly indicted and tried for murder. One was convicted of murder and two of manslaughter, and all moved for a new trial. A new trial was ordered for the defendant convicted of murder, and as to the other two defendants the case was continued to allow them to decide whether they would risk a new trial or abide by their convictions.[10] They were warned by Justice Grier:

> You ought clearly to understand and weigh well the position in which you now stand. You have been once tried and acquitted of the higher grade of offense charged against you in this indictment, the penalty affixed to which is death; but you have (escaped). . . . But let me now solemnly warn you to consider well the choice you shall make. Another jury instead of acquitting you altogether, may find you guilty of the whole indictment, and thus your lives may become forfeit to the law.

In a decision handed down December 16, 1957, by the United States Supreme Court, this long established rule was changed, and that Court set free a twice convicted murderer. The decision[11] dealt with a defendant who had been convicted of arson that resulted in a woman's death. Such an unlawful killing, in the perpetration of a violent type of felony, is murder in the first degree and, because the killing may not have been part of the felon's plan, is referred to as statutory murder.

At the first trial the judge, giving the jury instructions on *statutory murder,* inadvertently included instructions on *second degree murder.* The jury found the defendant guilty of arson and second degree murder. The defendant appealed and, since the verdict was based on the judge's erroneous mention of second degree murder the judgment was reversed. On retrial the defendant was found guilty of arson and first degree murder.

He appealed from his second conviction to the United States Supreme Court. The Court overturned the century-

---

[10] *U. S. v. Harding,* 26 Fed. Cas. 131 (1846)
[11] *Green v. United States,* 355 U S 184 (1957)

old rule. A majority of the justices held that his retrial was a second jeopardy and ordered him acquitted of the murder charge.

The dissenting opinion by Justice Frankfurter, joined in by Justices Burton, Clark, and Harlan, pointed out that the identical rule of law stated so clearly by Justice Grier was reaffirmed by the Supreme Court in 1905.[12] The dissent observed that continuously, until the current decision, Justice Grier's opinion had stated the rule of the Federal Courts, and *in the meantime Congress had made no change in the law.*

Perhaps the most striking aspect of this case is that it was not a matter of protecting a possibly innocent defendant: The *facts* underlying the verdict of both juries were (1) the defendant was guilty of arson, and (2) a woman was killed by the arson. The *verdict* of the first jury did not reflect doubt on those two *facts of guilt.*

But the aspect of fundamental import is that in breaking precedent the Court was legislating, not adjudicating.

------

12 *Trono v. United States,* 199 U S 521 (1905)

three

The Courts' Assault on
Personal Liberty

The hallmark of this republic has been responsible individual liberty—a revolutionary idea that enticed millions to emigrate from the old countries to America. Today however, to many leaders of thought, personal liberty is not a principal goal, let alone the nation's proudest goal. This attitude is reflected even among the judiciary. Discernable in the following three topics is the modern propensity of some courts to withdraw liberties that Americans have long taken for granted. These examples show court actions whittling down certain Constitutional guarantees until they are no longer recognizable as such.

1. FREEDOM: OF CONTRACT; OF ACTION. In organized societies the degree of liberty among human beings is measurable by the right to own and manage property, to buy and sell it, to contract. For nearly a century and a half American government made no deep, permanent inroads into this freedom of the individual American citizen. But 1933 saw the beginning of a chain of legal events that conceivably could lead to the destruction of the American hallmark.

The Agriculture Adjustment Act of 1933 was a long step down the road toward its possible destruction. Although this New Deal agricultural panacea was utterly foreign to our federal system of government and twice held unconstitutional,[1] eventually, in 1939, following a change in the personnel of the United States Supreme Court, the A.A.A. was upheld.[2]

At that time Justice McReynolds, joined by Justice Butler, protested that the Court had recently found the National Recovery Act, also a New Deal panacea, to be unconstitutional[3] for two reasons that were equally applicable to the A.A.A.:

First, that Congress possesses only the powers delegated by the Constitution.

Second, that Congress does not have authority to manage private business under the transparent guise of regulating interstate commerce.

The acute problem the A.A.A. was purported to solve

---

[1] *Butler v. U. S.*, 296 U S 1 (1936)
  Rice Mills v. Fountenot, 297 U S 110 (1936)
[2] *U. S. v. Rock Royal Co.*, 307 U S 533 (1939)
[3] *Schecter Poultry Corporation v. United States*, 295 U S 495 (1935),
  [the so-called Sick Chicken Case]

three decades ago is still with us. And it has become chronic. The A.A.A.'s total direct and indirect monetary burden is immeasurable and its resultant political distortions and economic dislocations cannot be approximated. In 1964, in fact, our glut of wheat led us to sell it to the U.S.S.R. on long term credit! As a by-product, the A.A.A. spawned Billy Sol Estes.

Enforcement of the A.A.A. presented serious problems, but it was greatly facilitated by a Supreme Court decision in 1937[4] that raised the "General Welfare" clause of the Constitution to the rank of a specific power of Congress.

The Welfare Clause had been much discussed while adoption of the Constitution was being considered. Madison, Jefferson, and other proponents repeatedly assured the electorate that the two words "general welfare" did not override specific provisions of the Constitution. To them the following words of the Constitution:

> Congress shall have the power 'to lay and collect taxes, duties, imports and excises, to pay the debts and provide for the defense and general welfare of the United States,'

meant that the national government could raise money *only* and spend money *only* to carry out its enumerated powers. They held it ridiculous to construe two words— general welfare—as superseding all the detailed allocation of powers and restrictions on powers of national government. They said the two words served merely to round out the terse allocation of specific powers, not to transcend the specific powers. The two words were unvaryingly so interpreted by the Supreme Court for the first century and

---

4 *Helvering v. Davis,* 301 U S 619 (1937)

a half of the nation's existence. The interpretation of the welfare clause having been established, its meaning was not properly subject to re-interpretation by the Supreme Court. Its meaning could properly be changed only by amendment of the Constitution. Nevertheless in the Helvering[4] case of 1937, sustaining federal old age pensions, the United States Supreme Court said:

> Congress may spend money in aid of the 'general welfare.'

These two steps, (1) holding the A.A.A. to be constitutional, and (2) holding the General Welfare clause to be a substantive part of the Constitution, cleared the way for invidious restrictions on the freedom of the American farmer. In its next step, the case of *Wickard v. Filburn*,[5] the United States Supreme Court ruled:

> . . . it is hardly lack of due process for the Congress to regulate that which it subsidizes.

If one concedes the constitutionality of steps (1) and (2), there is some logic in this holding of the Court. But the subject matter of the *Wickard* case should give pause to the citizens of a nation dedicated to freedom. In this case the Court sustained a penalty against a farmer for raising wheat beyond a quota set by the United States Department of Agriculture—on his own land for the sole consumption of his family and his livestock.

The decision was based on Article I, Section 8 of the Constitution that reads, in part:

> The Congress shall have power . . . to regulate com-

---

[4] *Op. cit.*
[5] *Wickard v. Filburn,* 317 U S 111 (1942)

merce with foreign nations, and among the several States, and with the Indian Tribes . . .

The Supreme Court found that these words conferred on Congress the power to dictate to this farmer how he might use his own farm! The reasoning by which it supported this almost infinite stretching of the Interstate Commerce clause was to the effect: *If farmer Wickard had not raised his own wheat for his own use, he might conceivably have purchased it from the channels of interstate commerce.*[6] It may come as a surprise to some that our civilization has now advanced to the point where do-it-yourself is un-American.

Some time later a similar case was tried by Chief Justice T. Whitfield Davidson of the District Court of the Northern District of Texas.[7] A Texas farmer, Evetts Haley, was being sued by the United States in a quasi-criminal action for raising grain in excess of a Department of Agriculture quota and feeding the grain to his livestock. In analyzing the case the judge reviewed the powers granted by the Constitution to the national government. He noted that some powers were granted to Congress originally; that some powers not originally enumerated, had been conferred later by amendment. He pointed out that Congress originally had no authority (a) to enact an income tax law, (b) to prohibit the manufacture or sale of alcoholic

---

[6] This extreme interpretation of the Interstate Commerce Clause was further expanded in the first Civil Rights Law decision, handed down December 14, 1964. In that case a restaurant owner, whose customers were local residents, was held to be engaging in interstate commerce because part of his food-stuffs came from out of state. *Katzenbach v. McClung,* 379 U S 294 (1965)

[7] *United States v. Haley,* 166 F. Supp. 336 (1958)

beverages. He then noted that requisite power for these purposes had been specifically conferred on Congress by amending the Constitution—The Sixteenth Amendment and the Eighteenth Amendment. But, he added, neither the original Constitution nor any amendment to the Constitution had conferred power on the national government to regulate agriculture.

On the basis of his finding absolutely no authority in the Constitution of the United States of America for the power claimed by the Department of Agriculture, the trial judge decided in favor of the defendant. But the Supreme Court of the United States ordered that the farmer be convicted. In so doing it did not find its action necessitated an opinion. The entire decision reads:

> Feb. 24, 1949. PER CURIAM. The judgment is reversed. Wickard v. Filburn, 317 U S 111

In these few words the Supreme Court reaffirmed its nullification of both the Ninth and the Tenth Amendments in the Bill of Rights.[8]

Americans have cause to wonder if the Supreme Court had surveyed the right-of-way it was opening by its "general welfare" ruling. Throughout all history invasion of the individual citizen's right to contract and to manage his own property has led down strange alleys; examples in

---

[8] AMENDMENT IX. The enumeration in the Constitution of certain rights shall not be construed to deny or disparage others retained by the people. AMENDMENT X. The powers not delegated to the United States by the Constitution, nor prohibited by it to the States, are reserved to the States respectively, or to the people.

recent decades are Communism in Russia, Fascism in Italy, and Nazism in Germany. In fact Italian Fascism is generally credited with introducing Socialism's Corporate State, the very hub of which is the curtailing of liberty. In extolling the system Mussolini spoke without apology of the subordination of liberty.

> We were the first to assert that the more complicated the forms assumed by civilization, the more restricted the freedom of the individual must become.

Although most of us are aware that the Corporate State type of Socialism was one of the major programs espoused by the Nazis, it is not generally recognized (and it may be worth the while of Americans to note) that, even in pre-Hitler Germany, the government had vastly curtailed individual freedom of action:

In *The Road to Serfdom,*[9] Friedrich Hayek states that as early as 1928 the central and local authorities controlled more than half (53 per cent) of the German national income. As a result, he points out, they controlled indirectly almost the whole economic life of the nation. In his opinion this made easier the rise of National Socialism and the "scientific" Corporate State.

Hitler himself viewed federalism as an obstacle in the path of the Nazi program. In volume II, Chapter 10 of *Mein Kampf* he wrote:

> . . . We cannot permit any single State within the nation to enjoy political sovereignty . . . National Socialism must claim the right to force its principles upon the entire German nation, and to educate Germany to its

---

[9] *The Road to Serfdom,* Friedrich A. Hayek, Univ. of Chicago Press, p. 61

ideas and thoughts, without consideration of the former boundaries of the federated States . . . National Socialist doctrine . . . has the life of a people to regulate anew, and therefore it must claim the positive rights to ignore (state) boundaries, which we reject.

Both Mussolini and Hitler claimed their programs would promote the general welfare.

Though it was not, of course, so attributed when presented to the American public, the New Deal's N.R.A. paralleled the Fascist corporate system of Italy. The N.R.A.'s companion act, the A.A.A., was similarly grounded on the state's management of business.

2. TESTAMENTARY BEQUESTS: A Philadelphian, Stephen Girard, died in 1831. In his will he left his fortune amounting to several million dollars to found a school for poor white orphan boys. The school, Girard College, was opened in 1848 under the direction of a board that included, ex officio, certain officials of the city. For more than a century Girard's endowment was regarded as a handsome, public- spirited disposition of his fortune.

One hundred and nine years after the founding of Girard College, the United States Supreme Court repudiated his will and decided[10] that the college must admit pupils who did not meet the donor's specifications; that it was discriminatory for others not to participate in

----

[10] *Commonwealth of Pennsylvania v. The Board of Directors of City Trusts of Philadelphia,* 353 U S 230 (1957). The benefaction specified by Stephen Girard's will was reinstated, at least for a time, by the substitution of private citizens in place of government officials as trustees. But Girard College is still under attack.

his largess. The ruling, of course, ran counter to the long stream of court decisions that have meticulously honored all but the most frivolous of testamentary directives. Certainly there was nothing frivolous about Stephen Girard's bequest to found Girard College.

The decision invites speculation as to the farther outposts of discrimination. So far there have been no decisions whether Girard's restriction to poor orphan boys is discriminatory against girls, or the non-orphaned. Nor is it clear—if Mr. Girard's money can furnish free education to 100 orphans, of whom only 50 may be white—why the closing of the college door in the faces of the other 50 white boys is not discriminatory against each of them who, except for the accident of being white, would have enjoyed the fruits of Stephen Girard's endowment.

3. WAYS AND MEANS: Appellate courts traditionally have confined themselves to accepting or rejecting a point of law.

It might have been predicted that, once our courts had broken out of the judicial compartment, they would experiment in legislative and administrative directives. And if they did so it was conceivable that they would from time to time hit the wrong target just as our legislative and executive branches have occasionally done. Congress and State Legislatures always have had difficulty in framing statutes that would accomplish their purpose or that would result in more gain than loss. Too often frustration or even tragedy has been the reward of well-meant legislative or executive action. Examples spring to mind:

In the legislative field:

—Prohibition would rank high among the flat failures scored by well-intentioned legislators.

—Congress stocked a museum with malaprop legislation in the early 1930's. Faintly remembered are its ill-fated efforts to grow north-south tree belts across the great western plains; the Resettlement Administration; harnessing the tides at Passamoquoddy.

In the executive field:

—By executive order in 1933 the President ended sixteen years of diplomatic non-recognition of the U.S.S.R. Researching the events of the ensuing thirty years, it would be hard to find a single 24-carat gain for the United States from this executive act. On the other hand diplomatic recognition cleared the path for a thousand Soviet gains: in theft of our atomic secrets; in loans of money, never repaid; in espionage; in propaganda; in Party organization; in prestige.

—The executive fiat of Roosevelt and Churchill calling for "Unconditional Surrender" was a dynamic pronouncement, but by withdrawing all incentive to Germans, Italians, and Japanese in positions of authority to overthrow their governments and to try to salvage something from decaying military situations, it hamstrung incipient revolts against Hitler,[11] strengthened Mussolini's position, and prolonged the war with Japan.[12]

One of the first lessons taught by experience is that

---

11 *The Struggle for Europe,* Wilmot, Collins, London.
12 *The Enemy at His Back,* Elizabeth Brown, Henry Regnery Company.

inspirationally conceived solutions often do not work at all, and sometimes aggravate the problem. It is therefore remarkable that erudite judges should take no heed of the inevitable hazards, unpredictabilities, and dangerous side-effects of sweeping new legislation, or of precipitant executive experiments. Three examples that follow permit no other conclusion:

(A) Considerably less than 100% success attended a legislative effort of the Supreme Court in 1954-1955. The goal of the Court's decision of the case of *Brown v. Board of Education of Topeka, Kansas*[13] was racial integration of all public schools,—an extension of rights to be enjoyed by some Negroes, and a curtailment of freedom of action of some Caucasians.

The decision is discussed later (Chapter VII) in detail, but the point of interest here is what the Court did accomplish and what it failed to accomplish. Its directive to the District Courts was that the process of integration shall proceed "with all deliberate speed."

In the many years following the Court's decision, a number of handfuls of Negro students were integrated into some schools of Northern and Southern states. While recognizing this, it must be noted that gains did not come without great losses. For example, the Associated Press of August 13, 1963, reported a tragic offset: Prince Edward County, Virginia, was threatened with entering its fifth year of no public schooling for either Caucasians or

―――
13 *Brown v. Board of Education of Topeka, Kansas*, 349 U S 294 (1955). This decision gave certain specific instructions to the lower courts, implementing the basic decision that had been handed down a year before.

Negroes, the latter numbering some 1500. The Prince
Edward County schools had been one of the parties in
the *Brown v. Board of Education of Topeka, Kansas,* decision handed down nine years earlier. Shortly after the
August 13 story, the AP reported an agreement whereby
private funds would make schooling available for the
ensuing year. But the four years without schooling for
so large a number of school-age children must be tallied
as a monumental setback.[14] Had the Supreme Court failed
to take into consideration the possibility of such adverse
results when, in 1954, it issued its with-all-deliberate-speed
decree?

Eight years after the Brown decision was announced a
single Negro was enrolled in the University of Mississippi.
In the following years token registrants were forced on
other colleges. Richard Wilson, in his syndicated column
of May 26, 1964, summarized the record of the first decade
following the Court's 1954 ruling:

> The percentage of Negroes in desegregated schools in
> 11 Southern states is calculated by the Southern Educa-
> tion Reporting Service at 1.18%—or 34,100 Negro stu-
> dents out of a total white and Negro school registration
> of 10,813,934. The figures in some individual states
> indicate how little has been accomplished. In Georgia

---

14 May 25, 1965, on an appeal from maneuvers by the parties and the
lower courts, the Supreme Court authorized the District Court to
take various steps, even to ordering the School Board or the State's
officers to operate public schools. Only the future can reveal what
educational results will flow from this decision. Justices Clark and
Harlan, both of whom had joined in the 1954 decision, dissented
from the part of the 1964 decision that held Federal Courts are
empowered to order the reopening of public schools. *Griffin v.
School Board of Prince Edward County,* 377 U S 218 (1964)

there were 177 Negroes attending schools with whites—
out of a total school registration of 1,026,857. In Mississippi integration does not exist at all. In South Carolina there were 10 Negroes in desegregated schools out
of a total school registration of 627,451. Arkansas, with
a total school registration of 440,035 has 366 Negro students in desegregated schools. As is the case in the District of Columbia, reverse integration has set in. Some
Southern and border state schools which were desegregated are now resegregated because of the white migra-
tion to the suburbs. This has happened to such a
marked extent in the District of Columbia that in
another 10 or 20 years there may be only a few thousand white children in public schools. What has happened in the South can scarcely be called token integration. It is not even the semblance of integration.
Where it exists it is a local phenomenon and it may
be generally, as it has been in a few cases, merely temporary. One conclusion is very clear. In a decade of
turmoil the Federal government has not been able to
enforce, even by the use of U.S. combat troops, the
integration of the public school system. How any edu-
cator can look ahead 10, 20 or 50 years and say that
the Supreme Court ruling will then be enforced requires an extraordinary gift of vision . . . All kinds of
tests have proved the federal power supreme, both in
the courts and at the point of bayonet, and yet integration of the public schools in the South has barely
begun.

Two results of the Supreme Court's action are clearly
apparent: In ten years the Court's 1954 decree achieved
personal educational advantage for only a tiny fraction of
the Negro population. On the other hand this, and other
racial legislation by the Court, underlay, sometimes di-

rectly and sometimes indirectly, in city after city,[15] in the North and in the South, a long series of ugly disturbances —with no end in sight.

It might be fair to surmise that the rising tide of racial friction would have brought disorders even without the Court's action. Or it might be surmised that, if the Supreme Court had not assumed to solve a difficult and emotion-packed problem, legislative action might have produced an acceptable evolutionary program, such as has characterized the nation's history.

The foregoing are mere surmises. But it is an undebatable fact that this drastic judicial action in the legislative field has afforded minimal relief to school-age Negroes.

(B) Six years earlier the Supreme Court had outlawed deed restrictions against the sale of real property to designated racial groups.[16] It accomplished this by a flank attack, the gist of which was that citizens could contract, but the courts would not enforce the contract. The presumable aim of the decision was to integrate the residences of Caucasians and Negroes.

Congress or any legislature facing such a problem would

----

15 Little Rock, Ark.; Greensboro, N. C.; New Orleans, La.; Oxford, Miss.; New York, N. Y.; Birmingham, Ala.; Cincinnati, Ohio; Boston, Mass.; Cleveland, Ohio; Cambridge, Md.; St. Augustine, Fla.; Brooklyn, N. Y.; Rochester, N. Y.; Jersey City, N. J.; Elizabeth, N. J.; Paterson, N. J.; Dixmore, Ill.; Philadelphia, Pa.; Selma, Ala.; Americus, Ga.; Tallahassee, Fla.; Covington, Tenn.; Greenville, Ala.; Orangeburg, S. C.; Springfield, Mass.; Bogalusa, La.; Jackson, Miss.; Los Angeles (Watts), Calif.; Chicago, Ill.; Long Beach, Calif.

16 *Shelly v. Kraemer*, 433 U S 1 (1948)

have approached it more professionally. It would have referred the matter to a committee. The committee would have held hearings and listened to testimony from voluntary or subpoenaed witnesses. From them it would have learned that the main cause of segregated living areas was not the inability of Negroes to move into areas occupied by Caucasians, but the Caucasians moving out; that many square miles of Northern cities would become integrated every year *if just half of the Caucasians* would stay where they had been living!

Having informed itself so far as possible, such a committee, and then the legislature, would have considered the practicality of statutes to remedy the situation. And the legislature would have been aware that, if a statute did not work as anticipated, a different solution to the problem could be sought or the statute could be repealed. Such flexibility is not a quality inherent in the judicial system.

The 1948 decision of the Court abridged one of the American citizen's most valued and valuable rights—the freedom to contract and the related doctrine of sanctity of contract. The goal the Court sought at such an expense has not been gained. *The Saturday Evening Post* of July 14, 1962, disclosed that fourteen years after this major dislocation of the law colored people and white people still lived in sharply defined areas in every metropolitan center in the North.

(C) In the third case chosen under the topic Ways and Means, a court assumed an *executive posture* in seeking an answer to a legal problem. The plaintiffs in the case were railroad workmen who were forced to pay dues to hold their jobs in a union shop. They complained their dues were being used to promote political causes to which they were opposed—obviously, as the entire court recognized, a violation of their Constitutional right of Freedom of Speech.

A judicial-type disposal of the issue by the Court would have been a blunt "No Trespassing." Instead, the United States Supreme Court, like an executive resolving a problem of policy, devised a formula solution. The Court suggested as a remedy for this invasion of Constitutional[17] rights that the six workers might sue for a refund of the fraction of the dues that had been diverted to the political activities of the union.

Justice Black was impatient with the Court's executive-type action. In this caustic dissenting opinion he advocated a traditional judicial disposition of the case:

> The First Amendment provides: 'The Congress shall make no law respecting an establishment of religion, or prohibiting the free exercise thereof; or abridging the freedom of speech, or of the press; or the right of the people peaceably to assemble, and to petition the Government for a redress of grievances.' . . . The stark fact is that this Act of Congress is being used as a means to exact money from these employees to help get votes to win elections for parties and candidates and to support doctrines they are against.
> . . . The Court's remedy is to give the wronged employees a right to a refund limited either to 'the proportion of the union's total expenditures made for such political activities' or to the 'proportion . . . [of] expenditures for political purposes which he had advised the union he disapproved.' It may be that courts and

---

17 *International Assoc. of Machinist v. Street,* 361 U S 807 (1961)

lawyers with sufficient skill in accounting, algebra, geometry, trigonometry and calculus will be able to extract the proper microscopic answer from the voluminous and complex accounting records of the local, national and international unions involved. It seems to me, however, that while the Court's remedy may prove very lucrative to special masters, accountants and lawyers, this formula, with its attendant trial burdens, promises little hope for financial recompense to the individual workers whose First Amendment freedoms have been flagrantly violated.

. . . The three workers who paid under protest here were forced under authority of a federal statute to pay *all* current dues or lose their jobs. They should get back *all* they paid with interest.

. . . A violation . . . however small, is, in my judgment, prohibited by the First Amendment and should be stopped dead in its tracks on its first appearance.

Not surprisingly, when a similar case[18] came up on appeal two years after the *Street* decision, the Court found it had to modify its *executive type* formula decision.

We recognize that practical difficulties may attend a decree reducing an employee's obligations under the union shop agreement by a fixed proportion, since the proportion of the union budget devoted to political activities may not be constant. The difficulties in judicially administered relief, although not insurmountable . . . etc.

It then tacitly admitted frustration in its executive role:

The instant action . . . has been before the courts for 10 years and has not yet run its course. It is a lesson of our national history of industrial relations that re-

---

[18] *Brotherhood of Railway & Steamship Clerks, etc. v. Allen,* 373 U S 113 (1963)

sort to litigation to settle the rights of labor organizations and employees very often proves unsatisfactory. The courts will not shrink from affording what remedies they may, with due regard for the legitimate interests of all parties; but it is appropriate to remind the parties of the availability of more practical alternatives[19] to litigation for the vindication of the rights and accommodation of interests here involved.

----

[19] Justice Black had suggested the Court had available a more practical alternative—a simple judgment for all the plaintiffs to be repaid all the dues they had paid, with interest.

four

The State and the Federal Republic

So it might be well to recall the opinion expressed by Daniel Webster, when the cornerstone of the Bunker Hill Monument was laid, in 1825: *'Our history proves . . . that with wisdom and knowledge men may govern themselves; and the duty incumbent on us is, to preserve . . . the cheering example . . . If, in our case, the Representative system ultimately fails, popular governments must be pronounced impossible. No combination of circumstances more favorable to the experiment can ever be expected to occur. The last hopes of mankind therefore rest with us . . .'*

If Americans now prefer to be governed from Washington, rather than to govern themselves . . . if (representative federalism is) lost here, as Webster warned, that system very likely goes forever. (Felix Morley;

Freedom and Federalism, page 145; Henry Regnery Company, Chicago.)

It is a simple fact of history that the "Thirteen Colonies" were independent nations at the time they adopted the Constitution and brought the United States of America into being. The Constitution itself was a contract under which each State surrendered some of its prerogatives of sovereignty to the National Government, and retained all powers and rights not so ceded. The States' reservations were specifically confirmed in the Bill of Rights by the Tenth Amendment:

> The powers not delegated to the United States by the Constitution, nor prohibited by it to the States, are reserved to the States respectively, or to the People.

Despite this guarantee, during the first century and a half of the nation's existence the sovereignty of the states suffered erosion from the outreachings for power of the legislative and executive branches of the national government. During this period, the judicial branch played essentially a passive role by its acquiescence.

But the traditional reserve of many American appellate courts began to give way in the late 1930's and a new direction was imparted to judicial action and thought. As the trend has taken form, the courts—no longer the mere endorsers of legislative sorties—have emerged as aggressors in cutting away the prerogatives of state sovereignty. Court-initiated invasions of states rights may readily be perceived at many other places throughout this volume, but at this point we will touch only decisions on four subjects:

1. Occupying the Field.

2. The Place of State Civil Law in a Federal Republic.
3. Downgrading the Legal Profession.
4. Gerrymanderings.

These are chosen because they demonstrate the directness and intensity of the drive by the courts upon state sovereignty.

1. OCCUPYING THE FIELD

Since acts of sedition are crimes against government, and since states are the bodies primarily concerned with law and order, almost all of them have laws defining such crimes. Many of the states enacted statutes in pre-World War I days to meet the threat of the I.W.W. and other violent revolutionary movements. In 1940 deep public concern over seditious activities spurred the national government, too, to enter the field with the Smith Act which has proved to be a valuable tool in protecting America against sedition. For fifteen years—years that included such exceptionally trying times as World War II and the Korean War—the Smith Act and the various state sedition laws coexisted without interfering with each other.

The coexistence of the criminal statutes was the status when, in 1956 an acknowledged Communist Party member, Steve Nelson, was convicted of violating the Pennsylvania Sedition Act. He was sentenced by the Pennsylvania court to twenty years imprisonment, to a fine of $1,000.00 and to costs of prosecution of $13,000.00.

Nelson's conviction and the Pennsylvania statute appeared to be in no respect extraordinary. Forty-two states, plus Alaska and Hawaii, had sedition laws, and the Smith Act itself was patterned on New York's Criminal Anarchy Statute. Congress has always provided that United States criminal laws do not supersede state criminal laws.

However, the United States Supreme Court reviewed the Pennsylvania judgment and reversed Nelson's conviction.[1] And it based its reversal on the ground that Congress had "occupied the field." In other words, the Court held that when Congress passed the Smith Act in 1940, it thereby voided 42 states' sedition laws, including the Pennsylvania Sedition Act.

By this decision the Court overrode three other interested governmental bodies: First, the Commonwealth of Pennsylvania that sought to protect itself against subversion; second, the Executive Department that was charged with enforcing the Smith Act; third, the Congress that had enacted the Smith Act. That the Court's decision in the *Nelson* case was counter to the wishes of its peers, the other two branches of the national government, was made crystal clear by Justice Reed, in a dissenting opinion which was joined by Justices Burton and Minton. First he quoted the Executive Department:

> . . . the Department of Justice . . . brief summarizes this point: 'The Administration of the various state laws has not . . . interfered with . . . the enforcement of the Smith Act . . . '

Then, with respect to the intent of Congress, he said:

> Finally, and this one point seems in and of itself decisive . . . The Smith Act appears in Title 18 of the United States Code . . . which codifies the federal criminal laws. Section 3231 provides: 'Nothing in this title shall be held to take away or impair the jurisdiction of the courts of the several States under the laws thereof' . . . The section was first enacted in 1825 and has ap-

---

[1] *Commonwealth of Pennsylvania v. Nelson*, 350 U S 497 (1956)

peared successively in the federal criminal laws since that time.

The decision of the Supreme Court added no whit of strength or effectiveness to the Smith Act. It freed Steve Nelson. It had a further effect in that it tended to remove some hundred thousand state law officials and police from any role in guarding against the overthrow of the Republic.

2. THE PLACE OF STATE CIVIL LAW IN A FEDERAL REPUBLIC

For every citizen the civil law of his state is an integral part of his environment. It is known to every informed citizen that the rules of law vary from state to state; that responsibility for order and fairness in governing rests with the individual states (except in the few areas ceded to the national government). Even the United States Courts, when no national issue is involved, resolve issues by applying the civil law of the state where the U.S. Court is sitting. However, in a United States Supreme Court decision handed down March 5, 1962, the prerogative of a state to determine the basic laws applicable to its citizens was brushed aside, as casually as if there were no such entity as a sovereign state.

Suit was brought in Pennsylvania courts against Allegheny County on a novel legal principle. The suit carried extensive implications. The proposed principle of law conceivably could cripple or retard the construction of needed public improvements, and might be ruinous to industry in the state. On the other hand, a citizen of Pennsylvania had suffered actual and severe damage; to wit, the residence of the plaintiff, Thomas N. Griggs, was under the approach path of the northeast runway of the

Greater Pittsburgh Airport. The bottom of the approved glide angle for approaching aircraft was 11.36 feet above his chimney. Planes taking off cleared his home by 30 feet to 300 feet; and on let-down they ranged from 53 feet to 153 feet above it.

The airport case obviously was a coin with two sides. Without doubt certain residents near the airport, including Mr. Griggs, would be substantially imposed upon by noise and fear of accident. But questions arise: While it apparently would be fair to allow damages to all landowners as badly situated as Mr. Griggs, should damages be allowed to landowners whose homes would be 400 feet, 800 feet, 2,000 feet under the passing planes? Or those not in one of the many paths, but as violently assaulted by the noise of approaching and departing planes? In other words, over what area would the conditions be acute enough to merit money damages? And what about the more distant property owners whose land was reduced in value although they could not collect damages? Were they to be twice injured by having their taxes increased to indemnify the closer landowners?

The proposed new principle of law, since it would involve millions of dollars, or possibly tens of millions of dollars, would unquestionably have political effects. It could become a major source of corruption. How could such a principle be phrased and administered to avoid the probability of some landowners collecting thousands of dollars for impairment of residential value, and later reaping a windfall in greatly increased industrial value of land due to its proximity to the airport?

What advantages or disadvantages might the proposed law have on the community in general? Would the ex-

pense force abandonment of the airport, and its transfer
to a more remote area where the cost would be bearable.
If so, what would be the effect on Pittsburgh, as a whole,
of being served by a less accessible airport? If the Commonwealth of Pennsylvania established a precedent of
allowing damages for airport operations, would that lead
to similar suits about express highways? Bridge ap-
proaches? Railroads? Manufacturing? Most comprehen-
sively: Would it be in the overall interest of the citizens
of Pennsylvania that the Griggs' claim for damages be
allowed?

Such considerations as these confronted the courts of
the Keystone State. Obviously they were difficult of decision—the great damage to the individual plaintiff's real
estate for residential purposes versus the injury the proposed new legal doctrine might inflict on the whole Commonwealth. Finally these were weighed by the Supreme
Court of Pennsylvania. The decision: Damages would
not be allowed. That decision by the highest court in
the Commonwealth should have settled that point of law
in Pennsylvania, subject of course to the power of Pennsylvania's Legislature to enact a remedial statute.

However, the United States Supreme Court reversed
the Pennsylvania decision.[2] It did so on the grounds that
the plaintiff's property had been taken *without due process of law.*

The grounds for the decision illustrate the *expansion
in semantic meaning* that characterizes so many modern
decisions. Frequently, as in the Griggs case, "due process"
is resorted to simply to substitute federal judicial conclu-

---

[2] *Griggs v. Allegheny County,* 369 U S 84 (1962)

sions for the judicial conclusions of the state courts. Semantically "due process" implies action that is not arbitrary; that is taken after due notice; that affords opportunity to be heard. In times past it has been so interpreted.[3] Admittedly Mr. Griggs had lost, but his case had been given consideration through the entire court system of a government a century older than the United States of America itself!

3. THE SUPREME COURT ATTACKS THE BAR

Throughout the entire nation individual lawyers and Bar Associations were taken aback by a United States Supreme Court ruling of April 20, 1964, on a suit brought

---

[3] "Due process," in recent years, has been given an expanded meaning, but the clear import of the words has traditionally been adhered to by the courts. Chief Justice William Howard Taft said, "The due process clause brought down from Magna Charta was found in the early state constitutions and later in the Fifth Amendment to the federal Constitution as a limitation upon the executive, legislative and judicial powers of the federal government, . . . The due process clause requires that every man shall have the protection of his day in court, and the benefit of the general law, a law which hears before it condemns, which proceeds not arbitrarily or capriciously, but upon inquiry, and renders judgment only after trial, so that every citizen shall hold his life, liberty, property and immunities under the protection of the general rules which govern society." *Truax v. Corrigan*, 257 U S 312 (1921).

In *Pennoyer v. Neff*, 95 U S 565 (1877), a decision known to every lawyer, Justice Field said, "every State possesses exclusive jurisdiction and sovereignty over persons and property within its territory. As a consequence, every State has the power to determine for itself the civil status and capacities of its inhabitants . . . to regulate the manner and conditions upon which property situated within territory, both personal and real, may be acquired, enjoyed and transferred."

by the Virginia State Bar. The targets of the suit were practices almost universally regarded within the profession as intolerable—"running, capping, soliciting, maintenance, and fee-splitting," activities that laymen would refer to broadly as ambulance chasing.

The suit was brought by the Virginia State Bar to stop a union's soliciting personal injury claims and channeling them to lawyers chosen by its own "Department of Legal Counsel." The ethical standards sought by the Virginia State Bar, and Virginia's statutory bases for the suit, paralleled those of most of the states in the Union.

The Virginia courts issued an injunction against the union. But the United States Supreme Court in a 6 to 2 decision[4] overruled the State's injunction, basing its holding on the guarantee of freedom of speech, petition, and assembly under the First Amendment of the Constitution.

As may be seen in a later quotation from the Court's opinion, its argument was hardly temperate. The facts of the litigation are well summarized in the dissent of Justices Clark and Harlan:

> By its decision today the Court overthrows state regulation of the legal profession and relegates the practice of law to the level of a commercial enterprise. The Court permits a labor union—contrary to state law—to engage in the unauthorized practice of soliciting personal injury cases from among its membership on behalf of 16 regional attorneys whom its president has placed on the union's approved list . . . the union, through its president, not only controls the appointment and dismissal of the approved attorney but also has considerable influence over his fees and often controls the dis-

---

[4] *Brotherhood of Railroad Trainmen v. Virginia ex rel Virginia State Bar,* 372 U S 905 (1964)

position of cases. Furthermore, from 1930 to at least 1959, the union had required these approved attorneys to pay to it a portion of their fees, usually 25%. Such an arrangement may even now be in effect through the ruse of reimbursement for investigatory services rendered by the union. This state of affairs degrades the profession, proselytes the approved attorneys to certain required attitudes and contravenes both the accepted ethics of the profession and the statutory and judicial rules of acceptable conduct.

In addition to denying the State of Virginia the right as a sovereign to regulate its bar, the majority of the Supreme Court of the United States uttered an amazing indictment of the nation's bar in general:

> Injured workers or their families often fell prey . . . to lawyers either not competent to try these lawsuits against the able and experienced railroad counsel or too willing to settle a case for a quick dollar.

Such an indictment, unless founded on almost undebatable facts, would be injudicious. What basis could the Court have for its charges? Certainly the indictment would not be supported by the appraisals of at least two classes of highly competent observers: (1) All experienced lawyers have learned that the bar abounds with attorneys who are able negotiators out of court, and dangerous opponents on trial. (2) Veteran trial judges, universally, hold the bar in high esteem.

4. GERRYMANDERING

Gerrymandering has been a conspicuous phenomenon of government in those two great exemplars of republican government, Great Britain and the United States, almost from their respective beginnings.

For those who have forgotten the date of the coining of the term "gerrymander," it was 1812. While Elbridge Gerry was Govenor of Massachusetts, his Jeffersonians juggled electoral districts so ambitiously that when an opposition politician, pointing to the outline of one district on a map, observed, "That looks like a salamander," it evoked the reply: "To me it looks more like a Gerrymander."

Elbridge Gerry, who had been one of the leaders in promoting the separation of the Thirteen Colonies from England and in the successful prosecution of the War of the Revolution, did more than furnish a handy label for a common phenomenon of politics. His own political fate demonstrated the technique by which Americans, with a reasonable degree of success, have dealt with extreme examples of gerrymandering from Colonial days to the present. Gerry had been elected Governor in 1810 and 1811. But his party's reapportionment in 1811 was so blatant a performance that it touched a sensitive nerve in the body politic, and Gerry was defeated when he ran again in 1812. His defeat demonstrated the fact that the power always resides in the electorate to punish political maneuverings.

"Gerrymander" as the term is used here: Gerry was concerned with increasing his power and his party's power in the State of Massachusetts; the salamander-shaped election district was merely a device to gain his end. Similarly in the following pages we shall be concerned with *goals,* and *purposes,* and *forces,* and *principles.* Many of the *devices* will bear no resemblance to Gerry's famous experiment in map making. As used in this discussion, therefore, "gerrymandering" refers broadly to any device for

using the machinery of government to maximize the power or influence of one or more factions, and to minimize the influence and power of opposing factions.

The chief performers on the gerrymandering stage are political parties, but there are many other interests concerned with having a voice in policymaking and with the placement of power. There are far too many of these to enumerate here. However, an elementary illustration of the principle underlying gerrymandering may be drawn from the early days of the development of the West, and the various groups that obviously were involved: cattlemen, sheepherders, farmers, pro-slavery factions, anti-slavery factions, cities, railroads, manufacturers, loggers, riverboatmen, hunters and trappers, canalboatmen, and more.

Every one of these groups had vital interests to be protected or advanced. In some instances these paralleled those of other groups, but inevitably there were points of conflict with each of the others. The relatively sound solutions of the problems posed by such competitors for power reflected the genius of our political system and contributed to the building of a great nation. Gerrymandering was very much the order of the day.

In more modern times, during the first half of this century, for example, the gerrymander continued to be ubiquitous. The most noticed effort was President Roosevelt's 1937 attempt to pack the Supreme Court. Opposition to this move, spearheaded by the nation's bar, swelled to impressive proportions, and the President's attempted gerrymander was defeated.

But previously—in a series of moves spearheaded by pay checks of the W.P.A.—he had succeeded in converting the

Negro vote of the North from an almost solid Republican phalanx to a redoubtable legion of Democratic Party strength.

He thereby undid an historic gerrymander of the Republicans: In the expectation that Negroes would feel an enduring gratitude toward the party that was primarily responsible for ending human slavery in the United States, the Radical Republicans in 1870 devised the Fifteenth Amendment and conferred the right to vote on the newly freed slaves. Their move was highly successful. Negroes were unfailingly loyal; an element of strength that helped maintain the Republicans as the dominant party for the many decades that elapsed before President Roosevelt took office.

Notable among gerrymandering efforts was Senator Wagner's National Labor Relations Act of 1935, which effected one of the most sweeping transfers of political and economic power ever accomplished without a physical revolution.

From such examples as these it is or it should be evident that the gerrymander is a perennial part of the American political scene, and that some of the problems underlying the phenomenon are among the most important, as well as the most delicate, in the functioning of this federal republic.

For over a hundred years the surging political forces of the nation were dealt with by its legislatures; during all these years the Supreme Court cautiously avoided the quicksands of "political questions." But we shall now examine four cases which illustrate that this restraint, this reticence, has come to an end. It ended with a decision handed down March 26, 1962 that cast doubt on the legality of Tennessee's formula for allocating seats for its Legislature's Senators and Representatives.[5]

The Court's break with its no-political-questions past was sharp, but the specific end sought by the Court was veiled—it sent the case back to the U.S. District Court for that court's attention, with no hint of what solution by the trial Court would be acceptable to the High Court. In successive cases affecting Michigan and New York it handed down similar non-committal decisions—a technique that obviously could not be continued indefinitely.

As the High Court's ends have gradually been revealed they suggest this is the most ambitious gerrymander in Anglo-Saxon history, and the one fraught with the greatest import to Americans. En route to its disclosure the Court struck a telling blow at Congressional supremacy, and denigrated the sovereignty and dignity of States of the Union to a degree unrivaled since the Civil War Reconstruction. In the initial cases the Court did not fully resolve the issues as they were presented; instead for two years it withheld disclosure of elective formulae that might be acceptable to it.

It may be many more years before the development of the Court's plan will be fully revealed, but an examination of the decisions affecting the first four states upon which the Court's new doctrine was impressed, will at least outline a process the Court is using to demolish State Rights.

The states were brought to bar in this sequence: Tennessee, Michigan, Georgia, New York.

---

[5] *Baker v. Carr.* 369 U S 186 (1962)

I. TENNESSEE: The Tennessee decision was on a suit brought in the U.S. District Court by Tennessee voters. Their complaint was that Tennessee's legislature had not reapportioned the districts represented by the 33 State Senators and 99 Representatives since 1901,[6] and that, due to population shifts, voters in their districts did not have proportionately as great electoral influence as the voters in other districts.

It may sharpen perspective in reviewing this case to look partly outside the frame of matters specifically discussed in the *Baker v. Carr* decision. For instance, the decision shows that the complainants were several voters suing on behalf of themselves and other similarly situated. This, of course, is a recognized legal device. But it is a justifiable and logical conclusion that the expenses of carrying the suit up to the Supreme Court were not defrayed by casual voters. Even a banker or a lawyer would indulge in the presumption that the suit was initiated and financed by some pressure group with a stake that would justify the great expense of litigation; in other words, that it was a *gerrymander* designed to increase the power of some factions and to reduce the power of opposing factions.

————

[6] Tennessee's Constitution called for reapportionment every ten years, commencing 1871, and it provided: that every county having a population of two-thirds of the ratio of 99 to the number of qualified voters in the state shall be entitled to one assemblyman (the Tennessee lower house has 99 members); that if two or more counties make up a senatorial district, they shall be adjoining and that no county shall be divided in forming a district.

On many occasions the Tennessee legislature considered reapportionment and directed various committees to study the subject, but the 1901 Act remained unchanged.

The political background of the State of Tennessee is worthy of note. In Civil War times, it was one of the Border States, violently torn between loyalty to the Union and sympathy with the Confederate cause. In 1864 it furnished, in the person of Andrew Johnson, Lincoln's vice-president and successor.

The State of Tennessee has been the principal individual beneficiary of the nation's investment in the Tennessee Valley Authority, and is the home of Oak Ridge National Laboratory (atomic energy). In recent times it has been represented in the Senate by such widely known figures as Cordell Hull (later Secretary of State), Kenneth Mc-Keller, Estes Kefauver, and Albert Gore. The Crump machine of Memphis ranks among the notorious city and county political organizations of the United States. Senator McClellan's investigating committee dwelt at length upon the tie-in of a Teamster's Union Local with municipal corruption in Tennessee. Political scandals in Chattanooga have received nation-wide attention.

In short, the state has never been a placid political millpond. Its citizens have historically contended with powerful crosscurrents of political forces. *Its voters have found it expedient to focus power in the rural areas and away from the faceless political machines that tend to proliferate in the great cities.*

When the Supreme Court abandoned its self-restraint on "political questions" in 1962, only 12 states had approximate pro rata representation in both houses of the legislature. The other 38 states—stressing representation of political subdivisions and geographical areas—could be said to exemplify the historic American system of representation.[7] The population of election districts varied greatly in colonial days—varied in post-Revolutionary days when the Constitution was drafted—varied at the very time of adoption of the Fourteenth Amendment—and varied continuously up to 1962—a total of three centuries.

And along with the vast majority of the states, Tennessee—without occasioning effective political repercussions among its own citizens—had chosen not to have pro rata numerical representation.

It was against this background of American and Tennessee history that the United States Supreme Court instructed a United States District Court that it should do *something*[8] about Tennessee election districts.

Dissenting opinions were written by Justices Frankfurter and Harlan each joining in the other's opinion. The following excerpts are from Justice Frankfurter's opinion—one of his last judicial labors before resigning from the Court:

> . . . In effect, today's decision empowers the courts of the country to devise what should constitute the proper

———

[7] In his syndicated column of November 5, 1964, Richard Wilson wrote: "As governor of California, Earl Warren saw the problem differently than as Chief Justice of the United States. He said in 1948, as governor, that he had never been in favor of representation in the California State Senate solely on the basis of population.

"'There was a time', he said, 'when California was completely dominated by boss rule', but that the state had been liberated from such domination. 'Our state,' he said, 'has made almost unbelievable progress under our present system of legislative apportionment. I believe we should keep it.'"

[8] The Supreme Court did not state what action the District Court should effect. It held, however, it should not have dismissed a suit by persons claiming their votes were debased and they were thereby denied equal protection of the law.

composition of the legislatures of the fifty States . . .
. . . The framers carefully and with deliberate fore-
thought refused so to enthrone the judiciary . . . if the
people . . . should ever think of making judges supreme
arbiters in political controversies, . . . they will dethrone
themselves and lose one of their own valuable birth-
rights; building up in this way—slowly, but surely—a
new sovereign power in the republic, in most respects
irresponsible and unchangeable for life, and one more
dangerous, in the theory at least, than the worst elective
oligarchy in the worst of times.
. . . The stark fact is that if, among the numerous
widely varying principles and practices that control
state legislative apportionment today, there is any generally prevailing feature, that feature is geographic in-
equality in relation to the population standard.
Examples could be endlessly multiplied. In New Jersey, counties of thirty-five thousand and of more than
nine hundred and five thousand inhabitants respectively
each have a single senator. Representative districts in
Minnesota range from 7,290 inhabitants to 107,246 inhabitants. Ratios of senatorial representation in California vary as much as two hundred and ninety-seven
to one. In Oklahoma, the range is ten to one for House
constituencies and roughly sixteen to one for Senate
constituencies. Colebrook, Connecticut—population 592
—elects two House representatives; Hartford—population 177,397—also elects two . . . These figures show
more than individual variations from a generally accepted standard of electoral equality. They show that
there has never been a standard by which apportionment can be measured.

Justice Frankfurter flatly denied the plaintiffs' basic
contention:

The notion that representation proportioned to population is so universally accepted that it is, in appellant's

words 'the basic principle of representative government'—is, to put it bluntly, not true.

On this note of disquietude Mr. Justice Frankfurter ended a Supreme Court career that had commenced in 1939.

five

The Gerrymander Marches On

It is important likewise that the habits of thinking in a free country should inspire caution in those entrusted with its administration, to confine themselves within their respective constitutional spheres, avoiding, in the exercise of the powers of one department, to encroach upon another. The spirit of encroachment tends to consolidate the powers of all the departments in one, and thus to create, whatever the form of government, a real despotism . . . If, in the opinion of the people, the distribution of modification of the constitutional powers be in any particular wrong, let it be corrected by an Amendment in the way which the Constitution designates. But let there be no change by usurpation: for though this, in one instance, may be the instrument of good, it is the customary weapon by which free governments are destroyed. (Washington's Farewell Address)

II. MICHIGAN: On April 23, 1962, the Supreme Court drove a wagonload of hay through the barn door that it had thrown open a month earlier by its Tennessee decision. The Constitution of the sovereign State of Michigan had been amended in 1952 to provide that the Senate of the State Legislature should consist of 34 members, each to be elected from a geographically described area (drawn generally along county lines), and further, to provide that the districts were not to be subject to change because of fluctuations in population. The amendment was adopted by a statewide *referendum*. The fact that there had been a referendum is worthy of special note, for a popular majority necessarily included the city dwellers.

In the Michigan courts the Amendment was attacked as being repugnant to the Equal Protection Clause of the Fourteenth Amendment to the United States Constitution. The attack was defeated in the Michigan Supreme Court, but upon the authority of its decision in *Baker v. Carr,* the United States Supreme Court sent the case[1] back for reconsideration by the Michigan courts.

Although the high court withheld any specific directive to the trial court, the remand clearly held that the citizens of a sovereign state are not the final arbiters of their format of republican government. Such a court ruling—one that overturns the expressed will of a majority of a state's voters on a political question—must rank as a gerryman-

---

[1] *School v. Hare,* 369 U S 429 (1962)

der[2] of a very high degree. What corroboration of the dismal forebodings of Thomas Jefferson!

It has long, however, been my opinion, and I have never shrunk from its expression, . . . that the germ of dissolution of our federal government is in the constitution of the federal judiciary; an irresponsible body, (for impeachment is scarcely a scare-crow) working like gravity by night and by day, gaining a little today and a little tomorrow, and advancing its noiseless step like a thief, over the field of jurisdiction, until all shall be usurped from the States, and the government of all be consolidated into one. To this I am opposed; because, when all government, domestic and foreign, in little as in great things, shall be drawn to Washington as the centre of all power, it will render powerless the checks provided of one government on another, and will be-

---

[2] Two years and two months later, in *Lucas v. Forty-Fourth General Assembly of Colorado* (377 U S 713), the Court spelled out in bolder type the scope of its gerrymander—a veto on democratic processes in the name of Democracy! The anomaly was commented upon by Raymond Moley in his syndicated column of June 20, 1965, "Colorado has not been so reluctant to change its representation in the state legislature as most states. In the 96 years since Colorado's admission to the Union there were, until the present imbroglio, seven major reapportionments of the legislature. One of these was passed by the state legislature; the others, under the initiative and referendum law.

"In 1962, the year when the Supreme Court began its reforming in the case of Baker v. Carr, citizens of Colorado placed two reapportionment proposals on the ballot. Amendment No. 7 provided that the lower house of the legislature be apportioned according to population, but that the upper house should be apportioned according to a combination of population and other interests. Amendment No. 8 provided that both houses be apportioned according to population alone. The voters of Colorado approved No. 7 by a vote of 305,700 to 172,725. They rejected No. 8 by a vote of 311,729 to 149,822. Not only did No. 7 win, but the majority of

come as venal and oppressive as the government from which we separated.[3]

The implications of the decision in *School v. Hare* are extensive. One month before, when the Court had sent *Baker v. Carr* back to the United States District Court in Tennessee without a specific guide, the Tennessee District Court Judge was faced with two problems: (A) Whether or not the Court should redistrict Tennessee? (B) If so, what the redistricting should be?

At that juncture, if the U.S. District Judge were tackling problem (B), he would have felt compelled to work out a jig saw puzzle that would allocate the 33 senatorial seats and 99 assembly seats in a way that was consistent with the wording of the Tennessee Constitution. But

---

voters in every county in which the plaintiffs in the case resided voted for it.

"Thereupon, the original plaintiffs challenged the constitutionality of the newly adopted No. 7. After an extended trial, the Federal District Court rejected the plaintiffs' case.

"The case was appealed to the Supreme Court of the United States. It reversed the District Court in an opinion in which Chief Justice Warren said in part:

" 'An individual's constitutionally protected right to cast an equally weighted vote cannot be denied even by a vote of a majority of the state's electorate.

" '. . . A citizen's constitutional rights can hardly be infringed simply because a majority of the people choose to do so.' "

Mr. Moley observed,

"After this, one might speculate that the court would invalidate the Dirksen Amendment, if adopted, because it had been approved by the U. S. Senate which is certainly the most obvious denial of the one man, one vote concept."

---

[3] Jefferson: Writings, Vol. XV, pp. 330, 331-2; Letter Aug. 18, 1821 to Charles Hammond.

then came the Michigan decision. It apparently told the
Tennessee judge (or any District Judge) to pay no attention to the Tennessee Constitution (or any other State's
Constitution). Something new had been added—or sub-
tracted—from the American system of federal government.

The quick and easy progression of the Court—one month
calling Tennessee's legislature to task for failing to obey
the State's Constitution; the next month demolishing
Michigan's Constitution—is a phenomenon every citizen
should note, and heed.

III. GEORGIA WAS NEXT: The third state brought before a
Federal Court was Georgia. A suit[4] was filed in the United
States District Court for the Northern District of Georgia.
There a three-judge court seized the new political power
the Supreme Court had created by the Tennessee decision.
On April 28, 1962, it outlawed Georgia's Neill Primary
Act of 1917 which had been in effect for two generations.

Georgia is amazingly subdivided into 159 counties, and
the Neill Act had carried forward a technique of county-
unit representation that had been conspicuous in the
state's governmental organization since Revolutionary
times. The complaint in the lawsuit was that voters in
the larger counties of Georgia did not have influence in
proportion to their numbers. Under the county-unit system the candidate receiving the plurality of votes in a
county would receive all of the unit votes of that county.
The eight largest counties had six electoral units each; the
next thirty in size had four units each; the remaining one

---

[4] *Sanders v. Gray,* 203 Fed. Supp. 158 (1962)

hundred twenty-one counties had two units each. This was the electoral system chosen by the sovereign State of Georgia.

Since the courts' rulings make Georgia's sovereignty no longer an adequate shield for its electoral practices, the question arises: "By what standard is Georgia's conduct unlawful?"

Certainly the unit system cannot be considered un-American. This nation came into being when 9 states, each acting as a unit, adopted the proposed Constitution of the United States of America. The Constitution not only provided for two senators from each state-unit, but also provided for the only total veto power, "No State, without its Consent, shall be deprived of its equal Suffrage in the Senate."

Amendment of the Constitution requires the approval of three-fourths of the state-units. The House of Representatives and the Senate each act as a unit. The President and Vice-President are voted for by electors who, as a slate, are elected by their respective states. If they fail to elect a president or a vice-president, the task passes to the House of Representatives where each state, as a unit, has one vote.

Nevertheless, the unit system of Georgia was struck down by decree of a court—a notable gerrymander, establishing a political system directly counter to the one that has served Georgians for many generations.

IV. THE EMPIRE STATE: Eventually there may remain no state in the Union that has not had its electoral system called into question. We might have stopped here in our review of the Court's plunge into trial of political questions, if it were not for the identity of the fourth state to be ordered to the bar—New York.

A pressure group consisting of a corporation and several individuals sued the State of New York.[5] Their suit attacked the validity of New York's Constitution and statutes apportioning seats in the Senate and Assembly. This action, also, was brought under the equal-protection-of-the-law clause of the Fourteenth Amendment. Dismissed by the United States District Court, as a political issue, the case was reinstated by the United States Supreme Court on the authority of its recent Tennessee decision. The Supreme Court ruled that:

> A justifiable federal constitutional cause of action is stated by a claim of arbitrary impairment of votes by means of invidiously discriminatory geographical classification.

The return of the action to the United States District Court to justify New York's format of government commands our attention because of the Empire State's notable contribution to the making of America. The state's history displays—on a larger canvas than any of her sister states—the factors that have made the America we know.

Undebatably the greatness that we and foreigners attribute to America is primarily the product of the day to day activities of the states and their citizens. The total credit, of course, goes to the federal republic; that is to say to the national government *and all* of the states. And although the national government has played important roles, its roles (as compared to those played by the states) have been minor in their contributions to this Union's

---

5 *W.M.C.A., Inc. v. Simon*, 370 U S 190 (1962)

greatness. To test this proposition (and using the State of New York as an example) it is only necessary to review the part the states have played in America's development:

The nineteenth century witnessed industrial, commercial, and financial revolutions that posed novel problems to the courts and legislatures of the states. Some of the problems were magnifications of pre-existing ones. Others were novel side effects of the remarkable and widely beneficial emergence of a dynamic capitalism. The legislatures of the various states rose to meet the challenge of these vast changes in society, and of the burgeoning new economy. In these endeavors the inventiveness and foresight of New York State's Legislature were invaluable, assisting and guiding the nation's quest on a score of points:

In 1811 New York's Legislature invented a General Corporation Law. Up to that time—to form a corporation, small or large,—it was necessary for the incorporators to apply to the state legislature. Each application involved the tedium, expense, and uncertainty that would be expected in enactment of a major change in a statute. But under New York's plan, incorporators need only tailor an application to comply with the statute. The law laid down the boundaries of permissible corporate powers, specified the management structure for corporations, and provided for incorporation by filing articles with the Secretary of State. New York's innovation cleared the way for the development of flexible business organizations that could keep pace with the inventiveness and vigor of the nineteenth century in America. All the states followed New York's lead; and the resulting evolution of corporations as workable business entities led to the most constructive utilization of savings that has ever been devised.

The banking function also loomed as a necessity of a thriving commerce. By trial and error the Empire State found a solution to this need. It first experimented in monopoly banking through chartering Alexander Hamilton's Bank of New York as the state's only bank. However, the resourceful New Yorkers, following the lead of Aaron Burr who got a *water company* charter for his Manhattan Company with powers so broadly phrased that it permitted him to operate the Bank of the Manhattan Company, successfully detoured that road block. In 1838 the Legislature enacted the Free Banking Act, which was quickly imitated by the sister states. New York's banking requirements were of such a quality that the state largely avoided the unhappy bank failure history that plagued many of the middle western states—and helped place New York City institutions in the role of bankers to the banks of the nation.

During the 19th century the insurance principle came into flower, and at the turn of the 20th century a New York legislative committee, with Charles Evans Hughes as counsel, investigated life insurance company practices. Its sensational disclosures attracted nationwide attention, and led to vast improvements of insurance laws, not only in the Empire State, but throughout the country.

Within the same decade many advances in the status of laboring men and women were recorded. Today these are popularly credited to labor unions, but the influence of unions was minimal in the decades when the basic protective measures were introduced—building and factory safety laws, Labor Department assistance to workers in collection of earned wages, and workmen's compensation laws. The credit for such improvements lay with the electorates and the legislatures. And New York State was in the van.

In the general commercial development of the nation, New York, along with her sister states, carried on in the tradition of the Common Law. This was a matter of utmost importance, as a strong case can be made for the proposition that the most valuable "natural resource" of this nation is its adherence to the inherited doctrine of *sanctity of contract* and respect for precedent *(stare decisis)*.

This proposition can best be argued by a comparison with the nations of Latin America. The one notable difference between us lies in the fact that we, of the United States, inherited and have consistently abided by the uncompromising *sanctity of contract* doctrine and the rule of *stare decisis* (that gave fixed guides to businessmen in the making of contracts). The courts' adherence to these two great principles encouraged Americans to put their savings to work as loans, or in joint ventures of varying complexity. And far more important, in the earlier days, led European citizens to speculate in the United States.

As such foreign *exploitation* proved extravagantly profitable, a veritable flood of European savings was invested in this nation helping to develop its lands and build its factories and railroads. The savage strivings of multimillions of dollars of capital funds brought competitive pricing and mushrooming business opportunities to the thrifty and industrious citizenry of this nation. And these opportunities beckoned more and more immigrants to this Promised Land.

The National Government had only a small role in the creation of the favorable investment atmosphere. Ninety-nine percent of the day-by-day enforcement of

contracts was the work of the three branches of the
colonial or state governments: the legislatures preserving
and refining the sanctity doctrine; the executives, including sheriffs, enforcing the law: the courts ruling meticulously on the basis of statute and controlling or persuasive
precedent. And continuously from Colonial times, on a
multitude of fronts, New York has been the single most
influential state in the Union. Even today a decision by
its courts is one of the most persuasive that can be offered
in the court of a sister state on a question that has not
been decided in that jurisdiction—a fact that is deeply
interwoven into the elaborate commercial fabric of this
nation.

So it may be said that New York has played the most
important individual role in the development of America.
But we cannot fail to observe that, while the Empire
State's part has been outstanding, it has not been unique.
The path it chose was not always the best, nor was it
always the one followed by most of the sister states. To
every one of the 48 states that eventually spanned the continent must be allocated credit for important contributions to the nation's evolution into a greatness that is
without precedent in all history. Each state has been the
innovator or among the first to adopt workable *modus
vivendi* and has made notable contributions to our cos-
mopolitan culture. In this symphony of the states has
resided the essential genius of America. An American
therefore may well be concerned about the results to
follow when the hand of the national judiciary is laid
on state after state. What will be the effect on the America of the future if the fertile interplay of the individual
states is to be crystallized into court devised patterns? Is

the thrust of the Supreme Court at Tennessee? At Michigan? At Georgia? At New York? Or is the thrust at America?

These judicial activities—with respect to Tennessee, Michigan, Georgia, and New York—led into a two year interlude that might be called an Era of Constitutional Hiatus; a two year period during which the public was informed only that which previously had been constitutional, was so no longer; a two year period during which Congress, and legislatures, and courts groped in the dark for formulas of representation that the United States Supreme Court would find not objectionable.

Almost overnight—following the Tennessee decision—the potentialities for gerrymandering through the courts became a fertile field of pressure-group activity. *The New York Times* reported on November 11, 1963, that 39 states had so far been brought to bar in 44 court actions. Since the earlier justices of the Supreme Court had kept the judiciary out of the gerrymandering arena for 173 years of the nation's existence, the question arises, "How did this change come to pass?"

In seeking an answer we might first take notice that the function of judging is unique among human activities. Most of the things that people do have a continuity, or a flow, but the professional acts of a judge are discontinuous: A dispute to which he is a stranger is laid before him; he renders judgment; he is through.

Although it is the judicial function to settle every matter in dispute, occasionally a decision fails to do so—resulting in a frustration of litigants typified by this parable:

Long ago, when an appellate court decision had left many disputed issues dangling, an exasperated lawyer moaned: "I ask a man with a watch, 'What time is it?' He doesn't answer me, so I turn to another man with a watch and say, 'I'd like to know what time it is, and that man over there wouldn't tell me.' The second man says, 'You're absolutely right. He should have told you what time it is.' "

The Supreme Court's first decision (1962, on legislative reapportionment in Tennessee)[6] was a he-should-have-told-you-what-time-it-is holding.

It was 1964 before the Court announced the type of appointment it demanded. Six states—New York, Maryland, Virginia, Delaware, Alabama, and Colorado—were affected by a group of decisions handed down June 15th,[7] the gist of the holdings being that both houses of state legislatures must have seats apportioned on an equal population basis, regardless of a state's statutes, traditions, or Constitution.

Four of the states thus denigrated had participated in drafting the Constitution of the United States of America and had been practitioners of representative government for a century before our national government was born!

If we examine the chronology of the reapportionment cases in reverse, a confrontation of puzzles emerges. Could men of the justices' learning and experience—when they were confronted with the powerful tradition against deciding political questions—have blundered into the Tennessee, Michigan, and New York decisions? Can it be that

---

[6] Page 64
[7] *Reynolds v. Sims,* 374 U S 802 (1964)

the equal-population-district formula was the intended goal of the Supreme Court's majority at every stage (though nearly two years elapsed, after the Tennessee decision, before it stated a somewhat specific formula)? If the Court knew its goal, why were the earlier litigants left dangling with he-should-have-told-you-what-time-it-is decisions?

Were the Court's acts merely stages of a public relations program that was planned to effect a sweeping change in the American federal system of government? And were its steps cautiously timed and limited so no great single stride might trigger an adverse public reaction? What ultimate aims did the Court have?

The only goal the Court has stated is distribution of legislative seats on an equal-population basis; a principle that has *never—throughout the centuries of successful practice of representative government—characterized the Anglo-Saxon nations.*

However, the results that flowed from the Court's deliberate pace suggest at least two other goals—goals of great magnitude. One may have been further aggrandizement of the Judiciary at the expense of the Congressional and Executive branches of the national government. The other may have been utter demolition of the federal system; a reduction of states to the status of mere counties, or administrative districts.

Was the latter end the court's true target? If that was the case, was the so-recently-discovered need to make election districts more "democratic" chiefly a tool for stamping out the fitful flames of State Sovereignty as being hateful Constitutional perversions? Perversions that

former Associate Justice Goldberg terms *echoes of nullification?*[8] If so, the campaign was as skillful as it was
effective, and as effective as it was skillful. By the time
the Court-desired voting formula was announced, the
American citizenry had been so conditioned to this form
of the belittling of states and changing the American system of government that the only newsworthy aspects of
the Court's fiat were the speculations of pundits on whether
the Republican Party or the Democratic Party would be
the principal gainers!

A report in *Time* magazine furnishes an illustration
of the way the public mind was conditioned in the two
years that passed after the Tennessee decision. The story
dealt with a decision[9] of February 17, 1964 in which the
Court issued its first specific directive on a standard for
legislative apportionment.

The article was excellently written and the facts were
presented without any apparent bias. But, as close reading
of the following excerpt will reveal, the gradual development of the Court's theme had impressed upon the writer
concepts of "constitutional duties" that were not in the
Constitution! And the reporter had just finished quoting
the very words of the Constitution!

> In a blistering, 29-page dissent, Justice John Marshall
> Harlan (with Justices Clark and Stewart writing sep-
> arate dissents) argues that Black was dead wrong. . . .
> He pointed out that Article 1, Section 4 of the Con-
> stitution says: 'The times, places and manner of holding
> elections for Senators and Representatives shall be pre-
> scribed in each state by the legislature thereof; but the

---

[8] Page 97
[9] *Wesbury v. Sanders*, 374 U S 802 (1964)

Congress may at any time by law make or alter such
regulations.' Moreover, Article 1, Section 5 says: 'Each
House shall be the judge of the elections, returns and
qualifications of its own members.'

The reporter continued:

Harlan recalled that in 1872 Congress passed a law
requiring that Representatives be elected from districts
of nearly equal populations. But that law was dropped,
almost unnoticed, in 1929. . . . Wrote Harlan: 'It cannot be contended, therefore, that the court's decision
today fills a gap left by the Congress. On the contrary,
the court substitutes its own judgment for that of Congress.'
That much was certainly true. But obviously neither
the Congress nor the many state legislatures *had fulfilled
their constitutional duties,* and their inaction led to the
glaring inequities in representation that the court now
is trying to correct. (Italics added)

It is fair to assume that—if the 1964 decision had not
been preceded over a period of two years by the series
of noncommittal decisions—the *Time* reporter would not
have editorialized as he did in the above italicised phrase,
for he had just quoted the exact words of the Constitution:

The times, places and manner of holding elections shall
be prescribed in each state by the legislature thereof,
but the Congress may at any time by law make or
alter such regulations.

That journalist, or any journalist, would have recognized that legislatures "fulfilled their constitutional
duties" when they prescribed the times, places and manner of holding elections. This Georgia's Legislature had

done. That journalist, or any journalist, would have noted that Congress fulfilled its Constitutional duty by either of two courses (1) by acquiescing to, or (2) by overruling the states' statutes—i.e., by action; or by inaction.

But the indoctrination had been so effective it led the reporter for *Time* into the profundity, ". . . obviously neither . . . had fulfilled their constitutional duties!"

six

Our Heritage: The Common Law

Law students are taught that our Anglo-Saxon system of law developed through three major phases: The Common Law, Equity Law, and Parliamentary (legislative) enactments.

The incomparable Common Law is distinguished by its doctrine of *stare decisis,*[1] commonly interpreted as "let the decision stand." This is quaintly defined in Bouvier's Law Dictionary:

STARE DECISIS (Lat.) . . . The rule is to abide by former precedents, stare decisis, where the same points come again in litigation . . . to keep the scale of justice even and steady, and not liable to waiver with

---

[1] Pronounced by lawyers "starry decysis."

every new judge's opinion . . . As it was said more briefly by Alderson, B., My duty is plain. It is to expound and not to make the law, to decide on it as I find it, not as I wish it to be.

It is commonly stated that *stare decisis* is not applicable to constitutional law, which is probably correct technically. However, the immeasurable practical value, both of *stare decisis* and of *enduring precedent on a constitutional question,* is that they enable a lawyer to say to a client, "You can do this. You can't do that." "Precedent" and "stare decisis" are used in this volume as synonymous terms.

Through *stare decisis* our British ancestors evolved an amazingly cohesive body of legal principles. But it had one obvious flaw—inflexibility.

As an escape from the rigidity of the Common Law, applications for more *equitable* justice were taken to the King's Chancellor, then as volume increased, to Courts of Chancery. This Equity Law was a fine palliative, but did not reach the root of the problem.

Finally, our great Anglo-Saxon system came into full flower in England with the invention of a legislative branch of government that could change or repeal existing laws, or enact new ones, as the legislature saw the need.

The British legal system was taken over by the 13 colonies, and later by the state and national governments. On this inherited legal system and two other foundation stones—the tripartite governmental form and our unique federal relationship—America in a brief span of years grew to an unprecedented greatness.

Except for glaring exceptions—initiated or countenanced by some courts of last resort—such is the American governmental format today. Attention here, however, is focused on the exceptions. There are many. And for Americans, aware of the magnificent historic achievements of their Nation, it is a proper cause for concern when some of their highest placed state and federal judges distort the basic American plan of government; usurp powers not delegated to them, or even specifically denied to them.

Properly speaking, of course, judges are not judges when they exercise powers not lawfully theirs; courts so doing are not courts. But be that as it may, when a certain court of last resort does unlawfully make a new law, it forthwith canonizes it. Its new law becomes a precedent that must be followed by all lower courts!

It is an anomaly of the judicial fiat that freedom from the binding effect of precedent is solely the self-conferred privilege of a limited number of judges sitting on the benches of courts of last resort. The thousands of judges of trial courts and intermediate courts of appeal still have to function under the age-old legal principles. Today's trial courts are as tightly fenced by *stare decisis* as were the trial courts of England's thirteen colonies.

Although many lawyers and judges, probably a majority, respect the Common Law and view it as one of the most important building blocks in the magnificent American structures of government, other members of the fraternity stand but little in awe of this institution. The latter are self-confident, articulate, and influential.

In today's speeches and today's writings of many commentators on government, including those of high placed judges, the old fixed points—the *stare decisis* of the Common Law and the constitutional compartmenting of our government— are treated as passé. Statutes and precedents are accorded no more fixity than they might merit if they were scraps of paper borne on a stratospheric jet stream.

Non-fixity has been extolled by a United States Supreme Court justice in a recent booklet, *A Living Bill of Rights*.[1]

A state supreme court justice has exalted the taking over of the legislative role by the judiciary. In a lengthy article[2] setting forth the excuse advanced for a high court's acting, extra-constitutionally, as a legislature, he characterizes *stare decisis* as a "rationalization" and an "ancient pretense," and assigns legislative bodies a subordinate law-making role. This is "modern" law.

The late Professor Karl Llewellyn[3] praised usurpation by the judiciary as the *Grand Style in American Appellate Judging*.

Since the desire of judges to be legislators is so conspicuous a development of the day, the following vignette is offered as perhaps throwing a beam of light on the

---

[1] *A Living Bill of Rights,* by W. O. Douglas, Doubleday, New York.

[2] "Ironically, judges themselves are all too ready to seize on this rationalization *(stare decisis)* to shift to others the responsibility for redressing judge-made bad law . . .

"For better or worse, the undoing is a notably difficult aspect of judicial lawmaking . . .

"There is in the ancient pretense *(stare decisis)* an estimable yearning for enduring law . . .

"However timely an overruling seems, a judge may still be deterred from undertaking it if there are cogent reasons for leaving the task to the legislature . . .

"What considerations make it preferable to leave liquidation to the legislature?"

Hard Cases Can Make Good Law, Roger J. Traynor, San Francisco *Recorder*, October 20-31, 1961.

[3] *The American Law Tradition: Deciding Appeals,* Llewellyn, Little, Brown & Company.

frame of mind of the judges who seek ever-increasing power for the judiciary.

Upon the induction of a new justice to a seat on an intermediate appellate court, a state supreme court justice[4] outlined for all appellate judges (who apparently were at one time unhonored, unsung, and confined to mundane judicial tasks) a new domain of "statesmanship." He spoke of a magnificently expanded realm now open to the erstwhile lawyers who gain seats upon appellate benches:

> The Bench, and particularly the Appellate Bench, needs able men. But ability alone is not enough. A good Appellate Justice *must be a statesman* as well as a judge.

The term *modern* is often applied to such trends in American government that have appeared during the last one or two generations. But the term needs to be carefully evaluated semantically. In some instances, *modern* has the connotation of "improved." If the reference be to modern locomotives versus those manufactured a century ago, the semantic implication is that the modern locomotive would outperform its predecessor in nearly every respect. By the same implications, a modern aircraft would be superior to the biplane flown by the Wright Brothers at Kitty Hawk.

However, the concept of improvement does not always adhere to the term *modern*. A *modern* painter or sculptor is not automatically rated as superior to Rembrandt, Michelangelo, or Rodin. Nor a *modern* writer as superior to Shakespeare.

---

[4] *Minutes of the California Supreme Court,* September 22, 1961.

Modern governments are not necessarily superior. The Latin American politicians and governments of the various nations that were formerly colonies of Spain or Portugal, might not be universally regarded as superior in political genius to those of ancient Athens and Rome.

It is proper to assume that the judges who trespass beyond the powers allocated to them consider modern principles superior to those they inherited. And they do not stand alone in their impatience with the American plan. From other governmental forums, from professorial desks, and from books and lecture platforms,[5] have come complaints about the restrictions of a "horse and buggy" Constitution. A popular phrasing is that *the achievement of national goals is more important than the niceties of Constitutional law.* Many voices complain of the checks and balances our forefathers wrote into our Constitution; of the clumsiness of the federal system; of the alleged shortcomings of government at the state and local level.

The way to radical change from the American system has been well paved by words:

A widely known proponent of Modernism, former White House adviser, Arthur Schlesinger, Jr.,[6] has said "There seems no inherent obstacle to the gradual advance

---

[5] Such speeches and writings often aver, or assume the American governmental form is a Democracy, a concept not expressed in the Declaration of Independence, nor appearing in the Constitutions of the Thirteen States, or the United States. By the same token the speeches and writings seldom, if ever, extol freedom, though it was the touchstone of the American cause; the most truly revolutionary idea since the advent of Northern European civilization.

[6] *The Future of Socialism: The Perspective Now,* Partizan Review, May-June, 1947, p. 231.

of socialism in the United States through a series of New Deals."

On January 15, 1964, President Johnson avowed broad Socialist aims (that were heavily implemented in the evolutionary Great Society legislation he drove through the 89th Congress), "We are going to take all of the money that we think is unnecessarily being spent, and take it from the 'haves,' and give it to the 'have nots' that need it so much."

Walt W. Rostow, State Department Policy Planner of both the Kennedy and Johnson administrations, in his book *The United States in the World Arena* (page 549) urged "an end (to American) nationhood as it has been historically defined."

The proponents of Modernism are not at all in awe of the world-acclaimed success of the American system. Unblushingly they propose radical changes in our governmental form. Unfailingly their "new" plans are but variants of the hackneyed, though indestructible, Socialist Utopia theories; theories, Americans should recall, that were known to and rejected by Adams, Washington, Hamilton, Madison, and Jefferson; theories, on the other hand, that for a full two centuries have furnished inspiration to a long, ever lengthening list of reformers that includes Rousseau, Robespierre, Marx, Engels, the Fabians, Lenin, Trotsky, Mussolini, and Hitler.

The planners' minimal deference for the American Constitutional plan is typified in the February 1, 1965 syndicated column of Robert M. Hutchins, former dean of the Yale Law School, former president and chancellor of the University of Chicago, co-editor of The Great Books, former deputy administrator of the Ford Foundation, president of the 20 million dollar Fund for the Republic which supports the Center for the Study of Democratic Institutions, author, and columnist. He proposes a constitutional convention as a means to effect sweeping changes "in view of what the Constitution leaves out, and in view of the fossilized character of its original features." He would uphold neither the federal relationship, nor the tripartite division of powers:

> . . . the states are a principal cause of our difficulties in coping with education, political parties and cities . . . Their chief function today is to handicap efforts to establish national standards and policies . . . The legislature does not legislate in any real sense of the word. The legislative program is the President's. And the task of keeping the Constitution up to date has been turned over to the Supreme Court.

And in his column of June 14, 1965, Dr. Hutchins cites approvingly a conclusion of his Center for the Study of Democratic Institutions that envisions an America very different from the nation today's Americans inherited; an America that would not lend itself to being extolled in any Fourth of July oration:

> . . . All countries have decided that education is the path to power and prosperity. At the same time, all countries have discovered that the period from birth to age 6 is so important as to be almost decisive in education. Hence all countries are showing a new concern about the conditions of preschool life. In the Soviet Union it looks as though the government had about decided to take no further chances with the family. . . . they look forward to the time at which all children will be in a school that permits them to be with their families only once a week and during vacations.

. . . the Soviet government, views the family with suspicion and wishes to diminish its influence. Any totalitarian regime, or one that is trying to break up the patterns of a traditional society, must take the same attitude. This is one of the reasons why some developing countries outside the Communist orbit are setting up boarding schools as fast as they can afford it.

. . . The evidence of the influence of the first six years on child development is persuasive. Their effects may perhaps be diminished as life goes on, but it seems unlikely that they can be erased. As education has become one of the major preoccupations of all states, they have to all become concerned with the conditions of early life.

The United States is showing the same concern. The American family of the future will either be a mere reproductive unit—and the family as we have known it is not really necessary for that purpose—or it will become a center of learning.

The new leisure that automation seems sure to give us may provide the chance to achieve this high ambition for the family.

Ambassador Arthur Goldberg, in an address to the American Bar Association at Chicago in 1963, advanced a proposition of such sweeping import that it deserves to be pondered by every citizen of every state in this Union. Although the speaker had then served for a few months as an Associate Justice of the Supreme Court, his words obviously reflect the views he had held as Secretary of Labor and as a member of A. D. A. (Americans For Democratic Action), whose membership so greatly helped to staff the Kennedy and Johnson administrations:

Re-assertion of the fundamental character of the Constitution, not as a treaty between the States, but rather

as a charter emanating directly from the people, is
ever necessary in the face of assertions, made even to
this day, that the States, or rather their legislatures, are
to be the final judges of their own powers and those of
the national government . . . These echoes of nullification are denied by the Constitution itself and by our
national experience. They have no place in our day
when our unity as a people is indispensable for survival.

Justice Goldberg's sloughing off the clear wording of
the Constitution and the Ninth and Tenth Amendments
is one form of today's attack on the federal form of our
government. A related technique is the suggestion of
changes that would finally and utterly destroy the federal
nature of the nation, leaving nothing but vestigial frag-
ments of local control over local affairs.

In the following quotation from *The Making of the
President,* by Theodore H. White[7] such suggestions are
strangely coupled with words extolling the Constitution
as "still" having "the quality of living genius." Mr. White
listed among the ends President Kennedy would deem desirable, abrogating the allocation of two Senators to every
state. Formerly this goal would have been outside the area
of rational speculation, but now—since the advent of the
1962-1965 doctrine of "democratic representation"—it is
conceivable that the two-senator allocation might indeed,
in due course, be done away with by a fiat of the Supreme
Court. In summarizing the problems of the presidency
as viewed by John F. Kennedy, Mr. White wrote:

There were Constitutional problems swelling in the
American system. So much of the old Constitution still
had the quality of living genius—but so much else was

---

[7] White: *The Making of the President.* Athenium House, Inc.

obsolete. How, for example, under the federal Constitution, could the federal government intervene in local government? . . . And how about a Constitution that admitted an Alaska (with 224,000 inhabitants) to senatorial equality with New York (16,500,000 inhabitants), that admitted a Hawaii (620,000 inhabitants) to equality with a California (15,500,000 inhabitants)?

Listing proposals for "modernizing" the American system reminds us that our federal republic, itself, is the product of revolution; that in less than two centuries its success has transported a new nation far beyond the horizons of forecast. The listing poses a challenging question: Are the modernists turning back the clock?

On the opposite side of the semantics of *modernity* are many lawyers and informed laymen who view the Common Law as an invaluable tool of our civilization, and as valuable today as it has proved to be throughout history. They hold that one of the keys of America's greatness has been its government form—tripartite and decentralized.

They believe the near-miracles, accomplished under the checks-and-balances of the America of an earlier and simpler day, can be repeated in coming decades on an ever vaster scale through the initiative of individual Americans. Their simple wish for all Americans, yet unborn, is that they may be free men and have the opportunity to lead meaningful lives. They view usurpation in America—whether by national government, an executive, a legislature, or a judiciary—as being not modern, but as archaic as the divine right of kings.

To the suggestion *the achievement of national goals is more important than the niceties of Constitutional law* they reply: Our forefathers, too, had goals; goals of such import to them that in 1776 they threw down the gauntlet to the greatest military power in the world. Our Founding Fathers had national goals—even to envisioning a nation that would span the North American Continent. Those architects of government did not view the Constitution as a grouping of niceties, but as *the* foundation for individual freedom; an indispensible covenant:

> In questions of power let no more be said of confidence in man, but bind him down from mischief by the chains of the Constitution. (Jefferson.)

seven

Precedent Abandoned

Some well-meaning people apparently believe that the judicial process rather than the political process is more likely to breed better solutions of pressing or thorny problems. This is . . . untrue to democratic principle . . . one of the current notions that hold subtle capacity for serious mischief . . . For in the end what would eventuate would be a substantial transfer of legislative power to the courts . . . a function more ill-suited to judges can hardly be imagined, situated as they are, and should be, aloof from the political area and beholden to no one for their conscientious conduct.
(From an address by Associate Justice John M. Harlan before the American Bar Association Convention, 1963)

From time to time in this country the desire of many citizens for a reform reaches so high a pitch that the proponents are intolerant in the extreme of any opposition; their immediate goal looms so large it tends to eclipse even the nation's basic goal—a government of law, not of men. Because of today's emotional atmosphere this chapter, touching as it does on the first school integration case, demands a brief foreword.

Many Americans merit the accolade, men of good will. It is, of course, only human for some Americans to appraise a given condition of their fellow men differently than others do. Further, men of goodwill may disagree, rationally, as to preferable courses of social or governmental action—or inaction. However, all Americans, for nearly two centuries, have operated the most successful instrument of human fulfillment that has ever been devised by man—our Federal Republic. Since this fact has for generations been granted by people all over the world, every American of goodwill should recognize that our Constitutional plan of government is of an importance transcendent to *any* individual problem at *any* time of *whatsoever* nature.

To an alarming degree, it is to be noted, this is not an accepted fact today. The march of events has been so swift, the pundits so plausible, the propaganda so effective that a constitutionally guided solution to a problem of today is widely viewed as outmoded—and it is so held by men who pride themselves upon their high quotient of goodwill. They regard the Constitution not as the rigid channel of government, but as a *repository* of *quotations* to be cited only in chosen contexts, and only to support or reinforce desired courses of action. Today, other men of goodwill, who believe implicitly in the precepts of the

Constitution, are subject to castigation for resisting solutions, or palliatives, which they fear may injure or doom the Republic. Americans indict fellow-Americans who cling to the Constitution's strict plan as man's surest safeguard of freedom!

The rapid change from strict constitutionality has been paced by judicial legislating, as was dramatically spotlighted in 1958 during argument before the United States Supreme Court.[1] The issue was the reasonableness of a proposed two-and-a-half year moratorium by the State of Arkansas in its school integration program. In his address to the Court, counsel for the State of Arkansas, Richard Colburn Butler, said, "Mr. Chief Justice, you've been the governor of a great state."

"But, I never tried to resolve any legal problem of this kind as governor," interrupted the former governor of California. "I thought that was a matter for the courts and I abided by the decision of the court."[2]

The Chief Justice's statement naturally introduces a flashback: When Earl Warren was governor of the State of California (and while he was district attorney of Alameda County, and attorney general of the State of California) the issue of law involved in the Arkansas case had for decades been resolved. Under a United States Supreme Court decision handed down in 1896 the course of action proposed by the State of Arkansas in 1958 would have been unquestionably legal. So when the Chief Justice referred to the decision of the courts he was not speaking of "the decision of the courts" that had existed during his

---

[1] *Cooper v. Aarons,* 358 U S 1 (1958)
[2] *New York Times,* August 29, 1958.

governorship, but of a decision that he himself, as Chief Justice, had written in 1954.

Before looking at the decision he had written and to which he referred, we might examine the law as it existed while he was governor. The law had been summarized in 1896 in an action affecting the State of Louisiana. The issue then before the Court was whether it was within the discretion of the Legislature of the State of Louisiana to order separate accommodations on railroad trains for colored and white passengers. (The legality of states maintaining separate schools for white and colored children had already been fully established by court decisions both in the North and in the South.)

The United States Supreme Court, relying in part upon the separate school decisions, held that it was within the discretion of the Louisiana Legislature to order separate travel accommodations.[3] Since the decision followed precedent it was not especially newsworthy. However, it did spell out the principle that in time was labelled "separate but equal,"[4] and in succeeding years was frequently referred to as the "leading case." In the 1896 decision the Court held:

> So far, then, as a conflict with the Fourteenth Amendment is concerned, the case reduces itself to the question whether the statute of Louisiana is a reasonable regulation, and with respect to this there must neces-

---

[3] *Plessy v. Ferguson,* 163 U S 537 (1896)

[4] Although the doctrine of separate but equal rankled many persons, both white and colored, it afforded one substantial advantage to Negroes: Where communities chose to segregate facilities, the Negro facility had to match the Caucasian facility. As a practical matter—to be certain of meeting the standard—proportionately more money was often spent on the Negro facility.

sarily be a large discretion on the part of the legislature. In determining the question of reasonableness, it is at liberty to act with reference to the established usages, customs, and traditions of the people, and with a view to the promotion of their comfort, and in the preservation of the public peace and good order. Gauged by this standard, we cannot say that a law which authorizes or even requires the separation of the two races in public conveyances is unreasonable.

The Court took notice of the historical fact that many Southern States for many years had legislatures composed mainly of Negroes, and recognized the possibility this might again occur in some states:

We consider the underlying fallacy of the plaintiff's argument to consist in the assumption that the enforced separation of the two races stamps the colored race with a badge of inferiority. If this be so, it is not by reason of anything found in the act, but solely because the colored race chooses to put that construction upon it. The argument unnecessarily assumes that if, as has been more than once the case, and it is not unlikely to be so again, the colored race should become the dominant power in the state legislature, and should enact a law in precisely similar terms, it would thereby relegate the white race to an inferior position. We imagine that the white race, at least, would not acquiesce in this assumption. The argument also assumes that social prejudices may be overcome by legislation, and that equal rights cannot be secured to the negro except by an enforced commingling of the two races. We cannot accept this proposition. If the two races are to meet upon terms of social equality, it must be the result of natural affinities, a mutual appreciation of each other's merits, and a voluntary consent of individuals.

The law as summarized in 1896 was a binding precedent for over half a century. Traditionally a court confronted with a case involving the same issues would have said in substance, "If this interpretation of the 14th Amendment is to be changed, it will have to be changed by Congress or by amendment of the Constitution."

Such a disposition was not the one chosen by the Supreme Court in 1954. Instead, as almost everyone knows, it ruled that maintaining separate schools for Negroes and Caucasians was unlawful.

The new law was made by the United States Supreme Court in a case entitled *Brown v. Board of Education of Topeka, Kansas*,[5] a decision that can be classified only as a usurpation by the judiciary of the legislative function. In announcing the newly made rule of law the Court said:

> The doctrine of 'separate but equal' did not make its appearance in this Court until 1896 in the case of *Plessy v. Ferguson,* involving not education but transportation.[6]

The Court then stated:

> In approaching this problem, we cannot turn the clock back[7] to 1868 when the (14th) Amendment was adopted, or even to 1896 when *Plessy v. Ferguson* was written.

---

[5] *Brown v. Board of Education of Topeka, Kansas,* 347 U S 483 (1954). This case is briefly treated in Chapter III of this book.

[6] Actually the legality of separate schools for white and colored children had been thoroughly established years before the *Plessy* decision, and many such cases were cited in it. Therefore what made "its appearance" in 1896 was the concept that facilities should be *equal* if they were *separate,* not that they might legally be separate.

[7] *The clock metaphor is counter to all sound rules of Constitutional interpretation. The United States Supreme Court said in South*

At no point did the opinion cite previous court holdings that were consonant with the conclusion it was going to announce. That is the cause of the deep concern expressed by many thoughtful American citizens over the school decision. Their concern does not arise from their feelings as to either the rightness or wrongness of separate schools, but from the Constitutional wrongness of an American court acting as a legislature. The United States Supreme Court is not vested with legislative powers. Its school decision was an act of legislation reversing an unbroken line of legal precedents dating back to the adoption of the 14th Amendment.

The 'authorities' upon which the Supreme Court based its opinion were solely the writings of certain sociologists. And while many private citizens might be in accord with

---

Carolina v. United States, 199 U. S. 437, "The Constitution is a written instrument. As such its meaning does not alter. That which it meant when adopted, it means now . . . Those things which are within its grants of power, as those grants were understood when made, are still within them; and those things not within them remain still excluded. As said by Mr. Chief Justice Taney in *Scott v. Sandford* . . . 'it speaks not only in the same words, but with the same meaning and intent with which it spoke when it came from the hands of its framers, and was voted on and adopted by the people of the United States. Any other rule of construction would abrogate the judicial character of this court, and make it the mere reflex of the popular opinion or passion of the day.' "

The distinguished and respected Judge Cooley stated in 1 Const. Limitations, 8th Ed., 124: "What a court is to do, therefore, is *to declare the law as written,* leaving it to the people themselves to make such changes as new circumstances may require. The meaning of the constitution is fixed when it is adopted, and it is not different at any subsequent time when a court has occasion to pass upon it." (Emphasis Cooley's)

See also footnote 4 on page 118

those writings, the Justices of the Supreme Court are not private citizens. Legislators, in framing statutes, might constitutionally give transcendent weight to such authorities, but only statutes and prior court holdings are 'authorities' for the guidance of judges. In short, such writings furnish no constitutional basis for judicial decision. Nevertheless the Court did reject legal authority and did adopt sociologists' conclusions as the only basis of an unprecedented interpretation of the Constitution of the United States when it said:

> Whatever may have been the extent of psychological knowledge at the time of Plessy v. Ferguson, this finding is amply supported by modern authority.*

*To the right is a facsimile of the authority referred to. It appeared as a footnote to the decision.

11. K. B. Clark, Effect of Prejudice and Discrimination on Personality Development (Midcentury White House Conference on Children and Youth, 1950) ; Witmer and Kotinsky, Personality in the Making (1952), c. VI; Deutscher and Chein, The Psychological Effects of Enforced Segregation: A Survey of Social Science Opinion, 26 J.Psychol. 259 (1948); Chein, What are the Psychological Effects of Segregation Under Conditions of Equal Facilities?, 3 Int. J. Opinion and Attitude Res. 229 (1949) ; Brameld, Educational Costs, in Discrimination and National Welfare (MacIver, ed., 1949), 44–48; Frazier, The Negro in the United States (1949), 674–681. And see generally Myrdal, An American Dilemma (1944).

Thus the Court overruled the law as it had been summarized by the *Plessy* decision, and all the decisions that had been made in reliance on it In the whole span of 86 years that had elapsed since the 14th Amendment was proclaimed there had been no single High Court decision as precedent for the 1954 rule. Therefore, this unanimous decision by nine justices of the United States Supreme Court stands as the most amazing deliberative act in the history of representative government.

One sequel of the 1954 decision is noteworthy at this point. Disingenuous argument has always been a characteristic of the philosophy that *the end justifies the means*. And obviously courts that legislate feel the end does justify the means. It is natural, therefore, that we should find examples of lack of candor when courts are embarked upon programs of legislation.

A lack of candor was detectable in the *Brown* decision of 1954. In pointing out that the *Plessy* case of 1896 involved "not education, but transportation," the Supreme Court (in legal parlance) was "distinguishing" these two areas of activity from each other. In effect the Court was saying, "We admit the law has been settled as far as transportation is concerned. But education and transportation are very different things, so we are free to make a different ruling with respect to education." That clearly was the import of the words "not education, but transportation."

But the 1954 distinction between education and transportation was short-lived. Step by step and case by case the Supreme Court moved ahead with its program of legislation-by-judicial fiat at such a pace that by February 26, 1962, it was able to decree in a transportation case[8]:

---

[8] *Bailey v. Patterson*, 369 U S 31 (1962)

We have settled beyond question that no State may require racial segregation of interstate or intrastate facilities . . . The question is no longer open; it is foreclosed as a litigable issue . . . prior decisions make frivolous any claim that a state statute is not unconstitutional . . . There is no such ground when the constitutional issue presented is essentially fictitious.

In a mere eight years the historic rule of law respecting transportation—apparently respected by the United States Supreme Court in 1954—had become "frivolous," and the issue "essentially fictitious"!

eight

The Dangers We Face

The succeeding chapters will touch on subjects that four decades ago would have borne no specific relevance to a critique on the law, but now defy omission, being brought to our attention by diverse factors: undermined checks and balances; aberrant currents of Bar Association activities; vying of courts among themselves to supplant established principles; assumption by the judiciary of a policy-making function. Our first attention will be directed to the breaking down of checks and balances; to a legislature and a judiciary permitting an executive to usurp their prerogatives.

As with every living thing, this nation is exposed to many mortal perils. One of the most dangerous is perversion of the constitutional plan. Huey Long furnished a preview of a possible overthrow of the United States Government—by free-wheeling fiscal policies and able demagoguery. From 1928 to 1935 his meteoric career and vivid political pyrotechnics, perhaps the most spectacular in American history, disclosed the quick inundation of constitutional government, as the levies of *checks and balances* were abandoned by judges and legislators. The like had not been seen before. It might be seen again.

Within two years of Huey Long's entry into the office of Governor, Louisiana was responding to the wave of his baton in total disregard of the metronome of constitutional government. The blandishments of his program, "Every Man a King," brought out imposing majorities at the polls. In the brief span of his political life, his Share the Wealth movement gained nationwide roots, and was already approaching full flower in states neighboring Louisiana, at the time of his assassination. Even the Federal Government, then at the floodtide of New Deal power, was refraining from overt acts that might antagonize the politically potent Senator Long!

Boldly spelled out for Americans during his reign was this sober fact: Constitutions and forms of government mean little when self-restraint is abandoned by one branch, and invasion of their allocated spheres is permitted by the other branches.

Although Huey Long just before his assassination in 1935 posed the most conspicuous threat to constitutional government on the national level, at other times and places oligarchy has replaced tripartite government to alarming degrees. It occurred on a grand scale in the post-Civil War period under the intemperate legislative drive of the Radical Republicans—a virtual dictatorship by Congress. Oligarchy is an omnipresent threat to municipal government: During the early 1900's the "Muckrakers" disclosed the breakdown of representative government in a score of cities.[1] In recent times evidence of such situations was brought to light by the McClellan Committee's disclosure that racketeers, collaborating with locals of the Teamsters Union, had taken over municipal government in such widely separated places as Seattle, Scranton, and Memphis.

While individual demagogues and entrenched political machines are ever-present dangers to Constitutional government, there are a myriad other visible threats. A wealthy, highly-organized underworld is among the many means by which our Republic could be destroyed. Earlier we cited the preoccupation of the courts with forgiveness of the derelictions of criminals as the motivation of judicial decisions that tie the hands of the police and public prosecutors. As this strange trend proceeds, its pace appears to quicken, and danger to the nation mounts.

Part of today's acute crime problem had its inception in Prohibition, the "noble experiment" that followed World War I. The results of Prohibition were far different and more far-reaching than its proponents ever envisioned. Criminal earnings achieved an enormity without precedent. The manufacture, transportation, and sale of liquor became big business. With bigness came *organization* and vast accumulations of illicit *capital*. Since then, under our high income tax structure, the relatively tax-free operations of crime and rackets have further swollen

---

[1] Lincoln Steffens, *The Shame of the Cities* (1904)

underworld capital. Underworld organization undoubtedly has kept pace. A hint at least of the depth and breadth of the organization of a fraction of the underworld was given by the recent "national convention" of Mafia leaders at Apalachin, New York[2] and it bespeaks an ominous inter-relationship.

In his syndicated column on January 24, 1964, Victor Riesel said that the official report of those present was not a fair count of the house:

> I have returned to Apalachin, N. Y., to the scene of the crime convention—and some startling facts still unknown to the nation.
>
> It was at the sprawling estate here of Joe Mario Barbara—replete with massive kitchens, walk-in deep freezes and a large fully equipped restaurant miles from any city—that Sgt. (now Lt.) Ed Crosswell on Nov. 14, 1957, surprised the leaders of interlocking syndicates who were conducting a crime cartel business meeting as though it were a gathering of insurance salesmen.
>
> Until this moment the country has believed there were 64 top syndicate gangsters here—all identified. Now it can be reported that there were between 100 and 120 master hoodlums and their retinues. This means that from 40 to 50 gangland leaders escaped, believing no one knew they were here . . .
>
> Despite the size of the delegations to the Apalachin cookout, the authorities now believe that there is a "ruling" national "commission" of only nine men, perhaps 12 at the most. This is far more than the Cosa Nostra operation described by Valachi. It is made up of men who are powers in their big cities or in regions of the country. The turnout at Apalachin was big

---

2 *United States v. Bonanno,* 177 F Supp 106 (1959)
  Bufalino v. United States, 285 Fed. 2d (1960)

because the "commission" summoned the lesser crime chiefs without first telling them the agenda. So each hoodlum of any consequence brought with him his own technicians, "bookkeepers" and bodyguards. The Justice Department . . . has collected vast amounts of data . . . on 1,100 criminal "executives" of organized crime syndicates. . . . The federals' target is the "commission," which it believes is made up of the following personnel: Sam Giancana, Chicago boss; Steve Maggadino of Lewiston, N. Y., a power in the big state; Joe Zerilli, a Detroit strong man; Vito Genovese, whom Valachi named as the Cosa Nostra chief; Joe Bonanno, of New York and Arizona; Tommy (Three Fingers Brown) Lucchese, behind the scenes "authoritative conciliator" living in New York.

There is the mighty tough Carlo Gambino of Brooklyn; Angelo Bruno of Philadelphia, now under indictment; Raymond Patriarca of Providence, R. I., and John Sebastian LaRocca of Pittsburgh.

Thus, the center of power of the big time syndicates appears based in the East. However, the two unknowns on the commission could represent the West.

Many of the "commission" members are in the labor rackets. According to a police official's testimony before the McClellan committee recently: "If there is trouble in a union and they are looking for goons or strong arm people to move in, Patriarca . . . would supply them." Patriarca, of course, is New England-based. There is no insinuation that the rule of the "commission" is absolute, or that it dominates all syndicate investments and rackets. There are the 1100 thugs in the lesser echelons. These men have power, too.

Not a day passes without the nation's press reporting some incident of violence attributable to the organized underworld, some even more grisly and threatening than the following samplings: *Time* Magazine,[3] illustrating the text of its story with a picture of two dead gangsters stuffed in the trunk of an automobile, said:

> American Tourists often have to explain to movie-going Europeans that Chicago is no longer the free-for-all shooting gallery that it was in Prohibition days. Well, not quite. In the past 17 months, there have been 25 unsolved gangland-style killings in Chicago, which is well below the record of 76 in 1926, but still in the classic spirit.

From Youngstown, Ohio on the day after Thanksgiving Day, 1962, came the story of a racketeer who was killed by a bomb wired to the starter of his automobile. The police identified this as the 82nd bombing in recent years connected to Youngstown underworld operations, none of which has been solved. That number of bombings would show a ratio of about one bombing to every two thousand inhabitants!

This amazing number of unsolved bombings points up a phenomenon common to organized rackets all over the nation—by strict discipline they seal the mouths of their members (and intimidate other witnesses of their activities) so effectively that the workings of the omni-present underworld are baffling to our diligent law enforcing agencies. In 1963-64 the long time frustration of the Secret Service, F.B.I., and others was clearly shown in their elation when in fear for his own life the little racketeer, Joseph Valachi, turned state's evidence and told about the New York organization he had served so long. From his testimony the public was afforded a glimpse

---

[3] June 1, 1962

of the ramifications of Cosa Nostra akin to checking a vast, dark warehouse from a balcony with the beam of a flashlight. And, as Victor Riesel pointed out, Cosa Nostra is only a unit of a widespread netherworld.

While the toll of crime in America mounts higher and ever higher, appellate courts are rendering successful prosecution of guilty criminals more and more difficult. They achieve this by infinite refinements on the technique of "trying the record" instead of trying the criminal.

From the earliest days the appellate courts of the states, except the New England States, have demonstrated far greater concern for the criminal than for the victim. William Seagle points out in his *Acquitted of Murder* (Henry Regnery Company, 1958) that the appellate courts of the states have reversed amazing percentages of criminal convictions. He cites reversals of 27.07%, 41.9%, 37%, 43.6%, 43%, 50%, 25.7%, 26.1%, 46.50%, 19%, 48%.

Now,—a relatively new development—the Federal courts are supervising state criminal law. At the time of the Sacco and Vanzetti trial in 1927, the Supreme Court was refraining from interference in state court adjudications. In the following years, however, this restraint was abandoned, so that today Federal interference is the most notable factor in criminology and is the major force in extending further immunities to criminals. And the wide sweep of criminal immunity is only hinted by the United States Supreme Court's action on 50 first-degree murder cases reviewed by it from 1935 to 1957. The judgments of the state courts were reversed or further proceedings were ordered in 31 cases, or in 62% of these reviewed. Over a third of the 50 were "confession" cases. In this group, the Court scored a 77.7% reversal record—14 out of 18 cases. To nail down this point of confessed murder, let us note that these reversals were granted to men whose guilt was known and proved; not to protect men who might be innocent of the crime.

As has been noted the words of a constitution or an amendment *speak as of the date it is adopted.*[4] Adoption of the 14th Amendment was proclaimed by the Secretary of State on July 28, 1868. The Amendment included a provision, ". . . nor shall any State deprive any person of life, liberty, or property, without due process of law."

While it might be difficult to state precisely what the

----

[4] At times (not consistently) the modern Supreme Court recognizes this proposition. In denying the right of the former Mississippi Governor, Ross R. Barnett, to a jury trial for alleged contempt of court growing out of his efforts to prevent the admission of James Howard Meredith to the University of Mississippi, the Court said, ". . . . our inquiry concerns the standard prevailing *at the time of the adoption* of the Constitution, not a score or more years later." (Italics added) *United States v. Barnett,* 376 U S 681 (1964).

The *Barnett* case also points to an incongruity growing out of the 1954 decision of *Brown v. Board of Education of Topeka, Kansas.* The basis for the 1954 decision was that segregated schools violated the equal protection of the laws section of the 14th Amendment. That Amendment also provides "The Congress shall have the power to enforce by appropriate legislation, the provisions of this article." If Congress, acting under the specific authority of the 14th Amendment, had passed a law and Governor Barnett allegedly violated that law, the Governor would have been entitled by the Constitution to a jury trial. However, it was not Congress, but the Supreme Court (and thereafter the lower courts) that "passed the law." The alleged violation being contempt of court, deprived the governor of a jury trial—truly a strange fruit picked from the tree of a Court that is jealous of the rights even of proven criminal recidivists.

See footnote 7 on page 106.

words "due process" did mean in 1868, it is possible to state some things they did not then mean. One thing that was not meant by due process in that year was furnishing free counsel for a defendant charged with burglary. In fact, in 1868, there was probably no court in any American city, county, state, or federal jurisdiction that had a requirement of free attorney service for a defendant charged with burglary.

During the ensuing ninety-odd years, by various techniques—some voluntary, some paid—in many state and federal courts indigent defendants have been furnished free counsel to represent them when they were prosecuted on some criminal charges. This was the state of things in 1963 when the United States Supreme Court decided that the *1868 due process of law* required that indigents be furnished free counsel in certain cases. The new rule, announced in deciding the petition of Clarence Earl Gideon,[5] attracted wide journalistic notice.

In the Sunday newspaper magazine, This Week,[6] George J. Jaffee wrote:

The greatest prison break of all time has quietly been going on for a year in the United States. Hundreds of prison-hardened criminals are walking out of their jail cells scot-free. Thousands of others will be freed soon. The most amazing thing about the great escape is that it's all legal, and due to a Supreme Court ruling.

The prisoners escaping are not minor criminals. They have committed serious crimes in 15 states of the U.S. In Florida, for example, a random sampling of the criminals released would include: A man, 36 years old, sentenced to 30 years in prison in 1961, for murdering his

---

5 *Gideon v. Wainwright,* 372 U S 335 (1963).
6 *This Week,* February 16, 1964.

girl friend with a pocket knife. A woman, 22, who had been convicted and sentenced in 1961 to five years in prison for armed robbery. A man, 28, convicted in 1960 to six months to life for assault with intent to murder. A man, 24, sentenced in 1961 to 20 years for armed robbery.

. . . in the 1963 Gideon case, the Court declared that a defendant must be furnished with counsel whenever any 'serious' crime is involved. Even this decision leaves open the question of a lesser crime or misdemeanor.

. . . Fifteen states were directly affected. Five of them —Alabama, Florida, Mississippi, South Carolina and North Carolina—had no legal guarantees of counsel for poor defendants except in capital cases. The other ten —Colorado, Delaware, Hawaii, Maine, Maryland, Michigan, New Hampshire, Pennsylvania, Rhode Island and Vermont—did not have a provision for counsel in all felony cases. Still other states, as Justice Clark noted, deprive poor defendants of counsel in many cases.

. . . Prior to the Gideon decision, Florida's state prisons held 8,000 inmates, 4,200 of whom had been sent to prison without representation by lawyers and who could petition for rehearing. As of December 31, for that 4,200, a total of 4,119 petitions for rehearing had been filed. To date, about 1,000 Florida felons—among them murderers and armed robbers—have been set free.

. . . It is impossible to tell at this point exactly how many inmates in the 15 affected states will be released. But there are straws in the wind which indicate that hundreds can be expected within the next year. Michigan expects many claims to be made. North Carolina has had over 600 inmates petition for review. About 20 per cent of these get a retrial. And in Pennsylvania, John G. Yeager, Director of Research and Statistics for the Bureau of Corrections, says, 'There has been a significant increase in the number filed.' At the time of

the Gideon decision, Pennsylvania had 6,400 adult
felons in its jails . . .

The prospect of thousands of convicted felons casually being released from jail is enough to give any
layman pause.

Time[7] said:

. . . In many cases where the courts have granted a
new trial, it is virtually impossible for the prosecutor
to rebuild the case—records and evidence are gone, witnesses have disappeared. (Florida) Judge Joseph Mc-
Nulty points to the pending case of a man sentenced to
life imprisonment in 1938 for second-degree murder
after being tried without a lawyer. 'He's pleading not
guilty, and it will be impossible to try him. The witnesses are dead or gone, and I'm not sure they can even
prove there was a corpse.'

The California Supreme Court[8] in 1965 reversed the
conviction of a murderer. It's action was based upon, but
went beyond, a United States Supreme Court[9] holding.

The defendant, Robert B. Dorado, had served time on
a conviction for the sale of narcotics; had been paroled;
was returned to prison for violation of his parole. At
San Quentin Prison about 8:00 A.M. on December 12,
1961, a prisoner, Nevarez, was found stabbed to death by
a short knife. Nearby in a trash can was a bloodstained
prison jacket with the name Dorado, and two short knives
with taped handles. A button missing from the jacket
was found near the body. In Dorado's cell were bloodstained trousers, and similar tape. After about two hours

---

[7] *Time Magazine,* October 18, 1963.

[8] *People v. Dorado,* 62 Cal, 338 (1965).

[9] *Escobedo v. Illinois,* 378 U S 478 (1964).

questioning, Dorado admitted the killing. The next morning he gave a written statement and led officials over the route he had taken in the course of the killing. Two days later he identified a fellow-prisoner, Jiminez, as the accomplice who held Nevarez while Dorado stabbed him to death with the short knife.

After stating this history, in detail, the decision said with reference to two officials who had participated in the questioning:

> On cross-examination, Captain Hocker was asked, 'Did you see or hear anybody mention to Mr. Dorado his right to counsel?' and 'Or his right not to incriminate himself or testify against himself?' To both questions, he answered in the negative. Mr. Midyett testified to the same effect.

It was upon the reply of Captain Hocker and Mr. Midyett that the Court predicated its reversal of the Dorado conviction.

The majority of the Court held that its decision was an implementing of Constitutional law.[10] Justices McComb, Burke, and Schauer dissented. Justice McComb

---

[10] The actual wording in the United States Constitution is: Amendment V, "No person . . . shall be compelled in any criminal case to be a witness against himself"; Amendment VI, "In all criminal prosecutions, the accused shall enjoy the right . . . to have the assistance of counsel for his defense." The Constitution of the State of California provides Article I, Section 8, "When a defendant is charged with the commission of a felony . . . The magistrate shall immediately deliver to him a copy of the complaint, inform him of his right to the aid of counsel, ask him if he desires the aid of counsel, and allow him a reasonable time to send for counsel; and the magistrate must, upon the request of the defendant, require a peace officer to take a message to any counsel whom the defendant may name, in the city or township in which the court is situated";

in his dissent said the Court's decision was unconstitutional:

> . . . Article VI, Section 4½, of the California Constitution . . . provides: 'No judgment shall be set aside . . . in any case, on the ground . . . the improper admission . . . of evidence . . . or for any error as to any matter of procedure, unless, after an examination of the entire cause, including the evidence, the court shall be of the opinion that the error complained of has resulted in a miscarriage of justice.' . . . An examination of the record in the present case leads me to the 'opinion' that there is no doubt of the guilt of the defendant . . .

The Los Angeles Times of December 10, 1964 carried this story:

SAN FRANCISCO (AP)

Forty-six men in San Quentin prison's death row will be among the most vitally interested parties Dec. 15 when the California Supreme Court takes a new look at two decisions which have helped keep the gas chamber idle for nearly two years.

On that date the court will hold a rehearing on the Dorado and Anderson cases.

The state attorney general and 55 of the state's 58 district attorneys say the original decisions threaten to free at least seven convicted killers and could release thousands now serving prison terms for various crimes . . .

Article I, Section 13, "In criminal prosecutions, in any court whatever, the party accused shall have the right . . . to appear and defend, in person and with counsel. No person shall be . . . compelled, in any criminal case, to be a witnesss against himself . . . but in any criminal case, whether the defendant testifies or not, his failure to explain or to deny by his testimony any evidence or facts in the case against him may be commented upon by the court and by counsel, and may be considered by the court or the jury."

Of the 46 men now on death row, 14 are under stay of execution pending future legal moves. The other 32 have active appeals pending or are awaiting new trials.

Immediately after the Anderson and Dorado decisions, three pending murder cases were dismissed by lower state courts before going to trial. The reason was that the only available evidence consisted of admissions made without the advice of an attorney. For the same reason, seven of the men on death row conceivably could go free.

Habeas corpus cases, from a low of 62 in the state last January, jumped to 335 in October from San Quentin prisoners alone. The favorite habeas corpus plea is the right-to-silence dictum of the Dorado case. The attorney general's docketing staff has been swamped by the load.

In asking and obtaining a rehearing, Atty. Gen. Lynch has been joined by more than 250 peace officers.

Two giant steps in frustration of criminal law enforcement featured the week of April 26, 1965.

On Monday the United States Supreme Court short-circuited the established channels of judicial review that previously led up to that court of final resort. In 1962 the State of Louisiana enacted two statutes in an attempt to protect itself against subversive groups that indubitably had and would make use of mounting racial turmoil to advance their particular goals. One of the laws provided that if a man were named in reports of the House Committee on Un-American Activities as a member of an organization, it was prima facie evidence that he did belong.

James A. Dombrowski, Benjamin Smith, and Bruce Waltzer, all officials of a purported civil rights organization called the Southern Conference Educational Fund were arrested for violating the statutes, and the organization's records were seized. Normally the case would have been channeled through the trial court and state appellate courts where the guilt of defendants and the validity of the laws would have been ruled on. Only after the state court review was completed would the United States Supreme Court entertain a petition to hear the case.

After their arrest the defendants sought to have the lower federal court restrain the State of Louisiana from prosecuting the case, but that court, invoking established principles, ruled against them. On appeal the Supreme Court by a 5 to 2 vote declared the Louisiana statutes unconstitutional.[11] The future ramifications of the Court's summary action could stagger the processes of law enforcement. Justice Harlan observed that states will have difficulty prosecuting under many statutes until the statutes themselves have run a gauntlet of federal review. He said:

> For me such a paralyzing of state criminal processes cannot be justified by any of the considerations which the court's opinion advances in its support.

On the following Wednesday, the United States Supreme Court overrode[12] the Constitution of the State of California on a provision that had been specifically upheld by the Supreme Court in 1946. The decision set aside the murder conviction of Eddie Dean Griffin, 54, an indigent Los Angeles Negro who was sentenced to California's gas chamber for beating Essa Mae Hodson, 49, to death in 1961. The battered victim was found in a

---

11 *Dombrowski v. Pfister,* 377 U S 976 (1965).
12 *Griffin v. People of the State of California,* 377 U S 989 (1965).

large trash box in an alley behind the apartment where she lived.

At the trial Eddie Dean Griffin did not take the witness stand, and Trial Judge Joseph L. Call, pursuant to the California Constitution,[10] reminded the jury of this. The District Attorney said, "Essie Mae is dead. She can't tell you her side of the story. The defendant won't."

The United States Supreme Court's decision superimposed the Court's amplified interpretation of the 5th Amendment of the United States Constitution onto California law. The 5th Amendment says simply, "No person . . . shall be compelled in any criminal case to be a witness against himself."

The Supreme Court decision effected a striking down of lawful comment on a defendant's avoidance of the witness stand in the States of Connecticut, Iowa, New Jersey, New Mexico, and Ohio, as well as California.

nine

Judicial Face

The preoccupation of courts with freeing guilty men suggests—in the oriental sense—that courts today are concerned with *face*. Applying the yardstick of *judicial face* —to the extent that occidentals can achieve an appreciation of oriental mores—may provide some explanation of modern trends that are otherwise incomprehensible to many American citizens. The pride the courts take in *face* may be gauged by the lyrical phrasing of their prose:

I think it is a less evil that some criminals should escape than that the Government should play an ignoble part . . .

Time out of mind, this Court has reversed convictions

for the most heinous offenses even though no doubt about the guilt of the defendants was entertained. It reversed because the mode by which guilt was established disregarded those standards of procedure which are so precious and so important to our society.

. . . Preserving and enhancing the fair name of law is always more important than sustaining the infliction of punishment in a particular case.

The common sequel to freeing vicious criminals is not difficult to surmise, but the following case history from New York throws it into bold relief.

In 1931, Frank E. Pendleburg, a delicatessen store operator in Queens County, New York was shot in the course of a holdup; he died in the arms of his wife who had come from their living quarters. The fatal shot was fired by young Michael Alex. His three companions were apprehended; they confessed, were tried, appealed, and were executed. After their trial, Alex was arrested and confessed. But when he came to trial, his three colleagues, as a result of their complicity in the murder that had been committed by Alex, had been removed from this world. There ensued a series of five trials of Michael Alex, no one of which was sufficiently free from "error" to satisfy the New York Court of Appeals.

Following the reversal of the fourth conviction of Michael Alex, (this time on a sentence of life imprisonment) he was released on five thousand dollars bail.

While he was free on bail he held up and murdered Jack Ehrlich, an insurance premium collector, from whom he obtained $16.45. For this crime, he did go to the electric chair. This leads to the query: What was the role of the New York Court of Appeals in the murder of Jack Ehrlich? Or of any Court in the fate of any future victim of any acquitted proved criminal? Or the composite role of all ultra-solicitous appellate courts (whose rules freed criminals) in the murder, robbery, beating, rape, maiming of a hundred thousand victims? The complacent phrases of the appellate courts ring hollow when they are requiem for a murdered man:

... the fair name of law

... standards of procedure which are so precious

... reversed convictions for the most heinous offenses

... less evil—than that the government should play an ignoble part

To some, the words of Jeremy Bentham, the English jurist and philosopher, would seem to be in point:

To acquit a criminal is to commit by his hands all the offenses of which he is afterwards guilty.

Michael Alex killed only one man while he was at liberty after the reversals of convictions. Sometimes society pays a considerably higher toll following the familiar conviction-sentence-reversal gambit: In October, 1957, Albert Anastasia, the Lord High Executioner of Murder, Inc., was dispatched by two gunmen as he sat in a barber chair in New York's Park Sheraton Hotel. He was credited by the police with the murder of 63 men; 31 personally, and 32 murdered on his command. Newspapers noted that he had been convicted in 1921 of first degree murder and sentenced to death, but had been freed after the New York Court of Appeals granted him a new trial.

A dramatic parlay of death occurred after California's

Supreme Court set aside the death sentence[1]—not the conviction—of a murderer. The high court held jurors should not be informed of a fact *available to any inquiring citizen* —that a "life sentence" does not necessarily mean a defendant will remain in prison for life. *The Los Angeles Times* of November 4, 1964, carried this report:

SLAYER SAVED BY TOP COURT GUILTY AGAIN
Convict's Escape From Execution Set
Precedent for State

A young convict who had been saved from execution by a precedent-shattering court decision last January was found guilty of first degree murder in Santa Ana Tuesday in the strangulation death of a fellow prison inmate. A jury of eight women and four men returned the verdict against Joseph B. Morse, 20, of Chula Vista, after deliberating four hours. The slender defendant heard the verdict without visible emotion.

Morse was saved from execution for the 1962 beating deaths of his mother and 12-year-old invalid sister by the State Supreme Court on grounds that his penalty trial for the double murder had been improperly conducted.

Ruling Retroactive

The court held that the jurors at his trial should not have been informed that he would be eligible for parole if he were sentenced to life.

Morse was said to have murdered Mrs. Hope Morse, 58, and Jennifer Morse to satisfy an "urge."

The so-called Morse ruling on Jan. 7 was made retroactive and affected the fate of 18 convicts awaiting execution in San Quentin's death row. Some of the cases are still pending.

Morse was sentenced to life on Aug. 7. A week later,

----

[1] *People v. Morse,* 60 Cal 2d 631 (1964).

using strips of cloth torn from a mattress cover, he garroted a trusty, Thomas Taddie, 23, of Boise, Ida., against the bars of his cell in the San Diego County Jail.

It is common knowledge that crime in the United States is on the increase, but David Lawrence made an arresting comparison in his syndicated column of July 25, 1965. After citing 503 American casualties in Vietnam in the last four years he wrote:

> . . . it may come as a surprise to learn that in a single year in the United States itself nearly 16 times as many persons—or approximately 8,000—were murdered.

Washington, D.C., which has been afflicted with an ever advancing ratio of violent crime, was the subject of a speech by President Johnson on July 16, 1965:

> In our land today no concern is more urgent to any of us than the increasing scope of crime and violence in the United States. There is no place where this malignant growth troubles us more than here in the capital city of Washington, which should be the model city as well as the capital of our nation.
>
> We know that Washington is not now a model for the preservation of peace and order. In fiscal year 1965, serious crimes in the capital city rose 12.4% over 1964. Since 1957, housebreakings have tripled, auto thefts have more than tripled, and robberies have almost quadrupled.
>
> Serious offenses rose 26.3% in June of 1965 over June of 1964. This June was the 57th consecutive month in which the incidents of local crimes exceeded that of the comparable month in the prior year.

The Supreme Court of the United States bears a substantial share of responsibility for Washington's booming crime rate in the opinion of Robert V. Murray, Washington's Chief of Police since 1951. The following is a question and answer interview with the Chief that was published in the October 21, 1963 issue of *U.S. News and World Report:*

Q. Chief Murray, Washington has a reputation for being a crime-ridden city. Just how bad is the situation?

A. Washington, like all large cities, has entirely too much crime. But of 16 cities with populations of 500,000 to 1 million, Washington was eighth in number of crimes, of all kinds, per 1,000 of population, in the first six months of this year.

Q. Did Washington rank higher in some types of crime?

A. In aggravated assaults, we ranked first. Those are assaults with a dangerous weapon.

Q. What about street crimes?

A. In robberies, which include those on streets—such as mugging and yoking—we were second.

Q. Is crime getting worse in the Capital?

A. Robberies and street crimes have picked up considerably.

Q. When did crime begin to increase in Washington?

A. Back in 1957 we had crime at its lowest point in 10 years here in the national capital. Then we had a certain court decision—the Mallory decision. After that, crime started to climb.

Q. What was the Mallory decision?

A. It was handed down by the Supreme Court. Andrew Mallory was arrested and charged with the rape of a woman here in 1956, and convicted by the District Court. The conviction was upheld by the District Court of Appeals.

Q. Was the conviction based on a confession?

A. Yes, it was. But about seven and a half hours elapsed between the time Mallory was brought in for questioning and the time of his confession and arraignment.

[Arraignment is the appearance of a suspect before a court official, where he is informed of the charge against him and advised of his rights] His case went to the Supreme Court, and the conviction was reversed because of that seven and a half hours.

The sole issue was the amount of time elapsing before his arraignment. There's never been any contention by Mallory or his attorneys that he was innocent, or that any force or duress was used to get the confession.

Mallory was released. A short time later he went to Philadelphia, broke in a house, and committed almost the same crime. He is serving 11½ to 23 years in a Pennsylvania prison. But that was under a state court. We are under federal criminal procedures here in the capital.

Q. What has been the effect of the Mallory decision and the ban on investigative arrests, in your opinion?

A. They have had a direct bearing on the increase in Washington crime. Three weeks after the Mallory decision was handed down, I testified before Congress that, in my opinion, the decision would have a very adverse effect on law enforcement here, and might possibly break down law enforcement. Looking back, I don't think I'm too far off on that.

Now let me go into a case. We had this 70 year old man who was struck in the face, knocked down on New Hampshire Avenue in the middle of the day—Sunday. The young thug went through his pockets and took what money he had. The victim went to the hospital.

Two days later a 54-year-old man was attacked in the same manner in the same neighborhood. The only description he could give was: "a young colored man, about six feet tall, wearing a gray sweat-shirt and khaki-colored pants."

One of our detectives spent some time in the neighborhood and soon found a fellow of this description hanging around. So he picked him up and took him over to the third precinct. Within 20 minutes, the suspect told the detective he had robbed both men.

The detective then took the suspect to the hospital—where the victim identified the assailant—and then to the home of the second victim, to see if they could identify him. But when the case went to court the judge said: "Why did you take this man to the third precinct?"

The detective said: "I wanted to question him about two assault and robbery cases."

The judge said: "Well, under the Mallory decision, you should not have done this. The cases are dismissed."

Now, how do the victims and the families feel about this? The cases were dismissed because two hours had elapsed between the time of the arrest and arraignment.

Q. Chief, how much has crime actually increased in Washington since the Mallory ruling in 1957?

A. It has increased about 50 per cent. You have to go back a few years to get the picture of crime trends in Washington.

In 1953 we had 23,918 "Part I" offenses. Those are defined by the FBI as criminal homicide, rape, robbery, aggravated assault, housebreaking, grand larceny, petty larceny and auto theft.

By 1957 we had brought these crimes down to 15,554. That was the year of the Mallory decision. Now, since 1957 we have added about 350 men to our police force, a K-9 corps [dogs] and additional equipment. We feel that, everything else being equal, we should have crime a whole lot lower.

But in 1958 we had 17,047 of these "Part I" offenses; in 1959—17,515; 1960—19,929; 1961—21,802; 1962—21,534. And I think that, so far, 1963 will show still another increase. I think it's going to increase as long as we have these restrictions on us.

We've also had a 14 per cent decline in the clearance of cases. Where we were clearing as high as 58 per cent of all crimes here, it's now down to 44 per cent.

Q. What does "clearance" mean?

A. It means solution of a crime. We call it a solution where a person is charged and the case is presented to a grand jury. Now he may, for some reason, be acquitted in court.

Q. Is it true that, under the U.S. Constitution, no one has to talk to the police if he doesn't want to?

A. Oh, that's right. Way back when I was a young policeman if we had a man and he said: "I want a lawyer" I gave him the phone book. But these restrictions we're faced with now are something new.

I'm in my 34th year with the Washington police department. I've got nothing to gain. I can't be promoted or receive any raises. But I do think that the public deserves better than they're getting in the way of these restrictions that are being placed on law enforcement. I'm not suffering from it, but the public is.

Q. In handling crime, do juveniles or adults give you the most trouble?

A. Well, a great deal of crime is committed by juveniles.

Q. Who is a juvenile?

A. Anyone under age 18. In 1962, in arrests for rape, 35 per cent were juveniles; in arrests for robbery, 33 per cent were juveniles; in arrests for housebreaking 34 per cent; in arrests for auto thefts, 46 per cent were juveniles.

Q. Are juveniles harder to convict than adults?

A. Again, we have a ruling here that I think is harmful. It is known as the Harley rule. Briefly, this prohibits the use of confessions, admissions and evidence obtained as a result of a juvenile's statements while he is in the juvenile status and before the juvenile court has waived jurisdiction.

In other words, say we get a juvenile in and talk to him about a crime or several crimes and gather evidence on him, get his statements, and so forth. Then if he's waived over to the adult court, all that is wiped out. We can't use it. It's just the same as the Mallory decision, you see.

Some of them have said: "You can't ask me questions. Don't you know about the Mallory decision?" Lots of juveniles have said this.

The young criminals who commit these serious crimes on the street—a great many are juveniles, but they're as big as any man in this room. They knock down people on the street and it is necessary to hospitalize them.

They are very defiant and arrogant, particularly if they've had any court experience at all.

We've had cases many times where we've had maybe two, three or four in a group who have committed robberies on the street—purse snatchings and what we call yoking of men, particularly elderly men. We would send the cases to court and the next thing you know, we'd pick the same juveniles up. Their first cases hadn't been called yet.

So I say that this makes them arrogant and contemptuous of law enforcement.

Q. How big a force do you have?

A. We have a force of 2,900 men. We have an authorized strength of not less than 3,000 men, but we have the appropriation for 2,900 and hope to get an additional 100.

Q. Is that enough—3,000?

A. I've been asked that question by committees of Congress that say: "Well, you need 500 more policemen." Well, 500 more policemen would help us, but that wouldn't be the answer to these restrictions that we have. I think if these restrictions were removed, a 3,000 man force could do a good job. Of course, I don't know any police chief who has ever said he had too many men, or even enough.

The *U.S. News* interview inspired an editorial in the *Washington Post* on October 17, 1963. The *Post* said in part:

To say that the Mallory rule creates crime is to indulge in a perfect example of what is called the post hoc ergo propter hoc (after this, therefore because of this) fallacy in logic. The police chief supposes that because the Mallory rule was devised in 1957 and because crime increased subsequently, there was a causal relation between the two. Crime has increased in every major American city since 1957. But among the 16 cities with populations between 500,000 and 1 million, Washington stood no worse than eighth in number of crimes of all kinds per 1,000 of population in the first six months of the current year.

One might just as reasonably contend that the crime rate rose in Washington after 1957 because that was the year in which the chief of police diverted his attention from law enforcement to lobbying for a change in the law.

Four days later—in its issue of Oct. 21, 1963, the *Washington Post* published the following letter from Chief Murray to the editor of the *Post*.

Your editorial of Oct. 17, 1963, entitled "Murray on Mallory," criticizes my response to the question, "When did crime begin to increase in Washington?" during an interview requested by the editors of *U.S. News & World Report*. My answer was founded on fact.

The national crime rate has increased steadily since 1950. In the District of Columbia, we were gratified that, while our serious crime (Part I offenses) reached a peak in 1952, the number of such offenses then began to decline until the low point was reached in 1957.

Beginning in 1957, our serious offenses in the District of Columbia have increased in number until we have now exceeded the previous peak year of 1952. These figures are substantiated by our statistical records, a graph of crime statistics clearly showing a downward trend to about June, 1957, and a steady climb thereafter.

I did not and do not say that the Mallory decision of 1957 is the only cause of crime in the District of Columbia. I recognize, of course, and have acknowledged that there are many causes . . .

I have long held that swift, sure punishment is one of the greatest deterrents to crime. I feel that a rule that diminishes the chance and opportunity to establish the guilt of an offender by proper interrogation will inevitably bolster his disposition to flout the law and law enforcement officers and, therefore, must have a causal effect on the increase in crime.

I base my statements on facts that I have learned in more than 33 years of practical experience in dealing with crime and criminals. I do not know what may be the basis on which your writer rests his charge that my position is 'a venture into sheer fantasy.'

It is true that for the first six months in the current year Washington stood eighth in the number of crimes per 1,000 in population, in the 16 cities with populations between 500,000 and 1 million. It should be noted, however, that, in 1957, we were in twelfth place. From 1957 to 1962, while serious crime in these cities, over all, increased by 21 per cent, it increased by 48 per cent in the District of Columbia, so that in six years we have moved up four notches.

Why Robberies Are High

This sharp trend is a matter of great concern to me. As a law-enforcement administrator, I am also disturbed by the fact that we stand second in the number of robberies. In the investigation of robberies, scientific evidence such as fingerprints is often not available, so that the proper interrogation of suspects, which in my opinion is impeded by the Mallory rule, is often vital.

In this connection, I must also notice the alarming fact that our rate of clearance of serious crimes has declined since 1960—in other words, we are clearing a smaller percentage of the crimes reported to the department.

I reject your suggestion that since 1957, or in any year during my career as a policeman, I have been diverted from law enforcement by lobbying activities. As the head of a police force charged with the protection of law-abiding citizens of the District of Columbia, I believe it is my duty to speak out clearly and honestly when questioned by congressional committees as to the reasons why the police department cannot cope with the rising trend of crime in our community. I shall continue to respond to requests to appear before congressional committees and I shall continue to testify honestly and frankly to the facts as I sincerely believe them to be.

I ask whether we must wait until Washington is first in crime before providing our police department with the right of proper interrogation which is possessed by other police forces throughout the United States, and which was available to our police force prior to the Mallory decision in 1957.

ROBERT V. MURRAY
Chief of Police

The preceding record of judicial leniency toward known felons could be amplified almost infinitely. On the other hand thousands of words have been written extolling the ultra-lenient attitudes of some appellate courts. Hence, it may be asked, "Is America's criminal law magnificent, or inept?"

As the *Washington Post* pointed out, somewhat complacently, crime has been increasing at an alarming rate all over the nation. But it is worth our noting that a statistical approach to crime, although of importance, can be confusing. The basic concern of society is with the occurrence of a crime—any crime—not with the ascending or descending lines on a graph of criminal acts. However, the mounting crime rate does tend to direct attention to some fundamental facts: First, criminal laws are written for the protection of society, not for the oppression of the criminal. Second, police and judges are supported by society neither to oppress, nor to protect violators of the law; only to administer the law. Third, their loyalty is due to the society that employs them; their duty is measured by the phrasing of the criminal law. How are our courts measuring up to their responsibilities under the criminal law?

Many criminals are not convicted, or not even indicted, because of certain safeguards; safeguards initially prescribed by society to avoid unconscionable oppression and the conviction of innocent persons. In numerous instances these provisions have been changed or expanded by the courts until no rational end of society is served by them; and the irrational expansion continues month by month. It is obvious that the rules of criminal law should be measured against the necessities of society. Chief among these are two propositions: (1) The rule that serves solely to minimize the chance of convicting an innocent man[2] is a laudable rule. (2) The rule phrased so bumblingly that it frees an unquestionably guilty criminal is a shameful indictment of the Statute's draftsmanship, or of the controlling decision.

Legal decisions cannot be reviewed *en masse*. Each decision stands on its own facts and the state of law then existing. But consider the situation where, because of some distorted rule of law, a court must order the acquittal of a criminal known beyond any reasonable doubt to be guilty. Too often the justice writing the opinion in such a case announces the decision with a complacency ill suited to the act's basic disservice to society. It would be fitting for any justice in such a situation to say: "It sickens me that it is my duty to turn you, a vicious criminal, loose upon society. However, such is the primitive state of our law, that, pursuant to my oath of office, I

---

[2] Author Erle Stanley Gardner, detective Raymond Schindler, Argosy Magazine, Publisher Harry Steeger, criminologist (and author of *Homicide Investigation*) Dr. Le Moyne Snyder, and lie-detector expert Alex Gregory collaborated for a number of years in defending or seeking executive clemency for men who were innocent of the crimes for which they were prosecuted. In a history of the operation, the *Court of Last Resort* (William Sloan Associates) Mr. Gardner states that one of the socially important facets of conviction of an innocent man is that it permits the perpetrator of the crime to remain at large.

have no other course. But I shall send copies of this opinion to both branches of the legislature with an urgent request that the problem be thoroughly studied and that the legislative branch attempt to make the law rational. I hope and pray the legislature can devise modifications of the law that (1) will offer the utmost safeguard to those who may be innocent, but (2) will protect other judges from such a shocking act as I am called upon to perform today."

ten

The Fourteenth Amendment
Versus Religion

It is a paradox of our times that the words "Constitution," "constitutional," and "unconstitutional" have
never been so freely employed as in these days when the
form of government envisioned by the Constitution of the
United States is being altered at an ever increasing tempo.
In large part the trend away from traditional American
government is based upon the 14th Amendment to the
Constitution of the United States as interpretation of its
terms has been progressively modified.

In the course of the United State Supreme Court's multi-
ple offensive against state sovereignty, in the spring of 1962

it forbade New York schools to have children recite the prayer:

> Almighty God, we acknowledge our dependence on Thee, and we beg Thy blessings upon us, our parents, our teachers and our country.

The decision,[1] one of the most vocally resented of modern times, was predicated on the part of the 1st Amendment to the Constitution of the United States that reads, "The Congress shall make no law respecting the establishment of religion . . ."

To the layman what the Constitution says *Congress* cannot do seems a far cry from saying what the *State of New York* can or cannot do. In fact the legalistic path extending from the enactment of the 1st Amendment to the Court's 1962 decision is not only a long, but a tortuous one.

Greatly foreshortened, this is the path:

1. It started where and when the 13 states that had won freedom from Great Britain decided to cede part of their sovereignty to a national government; one that was to possess merely the powers delegated to it in its constitution.

2. The draftsmen foresaw certain areas where the powers of the government they were about to create might tend to impinge upon the rights of the states or their citizens, hence the precise enumeration of national powers. And specifying such rights as trial by jury.

3. When the first Congress convened it performed as few such bodies have before or since: It initiated a Bill of

---

[1] *Engel v. Vitale,* 370 U S 421, (1962).

Rights—keynoted by the 9th and 10th Amendments[2]—to restrict the powers of the national government.

4. The Civil War came, ended, and was followed by the tempestuous Reconstruction. During this period the legislation we know as the 14th Amendment was proposed.

Its sections were so crammed with provisions lending themselves to any desired construction, and so hostile to the nation's federal nature, that it could only have been given serious consideration in the intemperate political atmosphere of those days. Sober arguments pointed to its dangers. Loyal and far-seeing men battled against it.

Ranged in its favor were the vengeful forces of the Reconstruction. They pushed the measure through Congress and then drove ruthlessly to wrest approval from the states. Felix Morley says:[3]

> The procedure was almost too preposterous for Secretary of State Seward, who on July 20, 1868, issued a very tentative proclamation of ratification. This pointed out that the legislatures of Ohio and New Jersey had, on sober second thought, repudiated their earlier ratifications, and that in Arkansas, Florida, North Carolina, Louisiana, South Carolina and Alabama, in that order, alleged ratifications had been given by 'newly constituted and new established bodies avowing themselves to be, and acting as legislatures . . .'
> Such back talk was not acceptable to the free-wheel-

---

[2] AMENDMENT IX. The enumeration in the Constitution of certain rights shall not be construed to deny or disparage others retained by the people.
AMENDMENT X. The powers not delegated to the United States by the Constitution, nor prohibited by it to the States, are reserved to the States respectively, or to the people.

[3] Felix Morley, *Freedom and Federalism*, page 80, Henry Regnery Company, Chicago.

ing Radicals. The following day they jammed through a concurrent resolution asserting that the Amendment had been ratified by twenty-nine States, including those questioned by Seward, and ordering him to promulgate it as a part of the Constitution. On July 28, the Secretary of State did so, in a statement which made clear he was acting by command of Congress.

Up until the day the proposed amendment was so hesitantly proclaimed by the Secretary of State to be the 14th Amendment to the Constitution, astute citizens warned that its provisions posed insidious dangers for free Americans. Immediately after the proclamation a question whether the document ever legally became an Amendment to the Constitution flamed up, and has flared or smoldered ever since. The validity of the forebodings of the Amendments' opponents and the record of the uses to which it was put, were placed in this capsule of appraisal by Dr. Harry Elmer Barnes:[4]

> The Fourteenth Amendment to our Federal Constitution, in connection with the power of the Supreme Court to declare Federal laws unconstitutional, provided the most ingenious instrument in all human history for social and economic exploitation in the name of freedom and liberty.

5. The most sweeping question ever presented to the Court was the challenge that the 14th Amendment was not legally enacted. Historically the Supreme Court has declined the issue, basing its refusal on the ground of avoiding political questions.

While declining to rule on the issue as such, the Court

---

[4] Barnes, A. Survey of Western Civilization, p. 874, Thomas Y. Crowell, New York

has accepted the 14th Amendment as a part of the Constitution, and it underlies directly or indirectly, a vast fraction of the controversies that are allowed by the Court to come before it.

6. It is a truism that the instinct of human beings, at all levels of endeavor, is to exercise power if the tools for so doing are conveniently available. The 14th Amendment was such a tool. Even before the judicial expansion of recent decades the Supreme Court invoked the 14th Amendment to impute the restrictions of the Bill of Rights to the states—an expansion of the power of the federal judiciary that rivals the 14th Amendment itself.

Thus it is that the United States Supreme Court found it had jurisdiction to review the New York courts' orders that had sustained the school prayer.

The issue: Did the school prayer violate the 1st Amendment words "The Congress shall make no law respecting an establishment of religion?"

Some sharp divergences of opinion between conscientious citizens have developed over the advisability and propriety of the New York prayer, but the issue before the Supreme Court was narrower—did the school prayer run counter to the words of the 1st Amendment? Admittedly one of today's Marxist-Nihilists would view any group acknowledgment of a Supreme Being as "an establishment of religion," but his view could not serve as a yardstick for the Court. Its yardstick must be the meaning of the words in America at the close of the 18th Century; in America in 1790[5] did "an establishment of re-

---

[5] A constitution (in this instance the 1st Amendment) speaks as of the date of enactment. See footnote 7 on page 106.

ligion" mean anything but a specific denomination: Church of England; Roman Catholic; Greek Catholic? By a vote of 6 to 1 the Court held the prayer to be unconstitutional.

Subsequent developments point to grave, far-reaching dangers to our tripartite government. The Supreme Court applied its "religious freedom" doctrine again in 1963, and again the public was aroused. In the summer of that year a UPI survey[6] reported that affirmative directives for religious exercises has been issued by school superintendent of Montague, a town of northwestern Massachusetts, and of the states of Georgia and South Carolina; by the school boards of Mahwah, New Jersey, and of the states of Kentucky and Alabama; by the legislature of the State of Florida.

The widespread defiance poses a question: How will the Court make its religious freedom doctrine effective?

It is true we have seen two presidents go so far in support of Supreme Court decisions as to strain or exceed their own Constitutional powers in ordering out the Army to enforce registration of Negro students. The Bible-reading controversies, however, have very different (dangerous) political overtones. It is highly improbable, in fact, almost inconceivable, that any president would send soldiers to restrain school teachers, or that any president's Attorney General would prosecute them for criminal contempt for reading a Bible passage to school children.

Because our courts have no built-in power to enforce their decrees, their authority has always rested on an intangible—the habit of accepting the judicial decision. This

---

[6] August 7, 1963.

almost unquestioned acquiesence to court decisions has been of inestimable value to our civilization. The habit dates back to colonial times. But recently many thoughtful citizens have been concerned lest a long continued pattern of judicial overreaching might backfire and destroy the delicate machine of judicial authority. If such foreboding should become fact, and the functioning of the judicial branch of government should be impaired, American civilization would suffer a deep and dangerous wound.

eleven

Obliviousness and Dangers

In some modern judicial thinking, various branches of *social sciences* receive more attention than *legal precedent*. For instance, *political forecasting* underlies many court decisions of recent years:

In 1961 the State Bars of two states, Illinois and California, were upheld by the United States Supreme Court in their refusals to admit lawyer-applicants who refused to say whether they had been Communists.[1] This decision was the last time, up to this writing, in which a majority of the Court has exhibited wariness about the

---

[1] *Konigsberg v. State Bar of California,* 366 U S 36 (1961)
  Companion case: *Anastaplo v. State Bar of Illinois,* 366 U S 82 (1961)

enmity of the Communist Party toward the United States.

Since then[2] the Court has frustrated many attempts to control the Communist apparatus; or to prosecute its members for subversive action. And the Court's 1961 action was a 5 to 4 decision. Because the opinion of this minority of four summarizes a philosophy that apparently has guided the Court since 1961 in many of its decisions, it merits consideration. The minority opinion said in part:

> And I believe the abridgment of liberty here, as in most of the other cases in that line, is based upon nothing more than a fear that the American people can be alienated from their allegiance to our form of government by the talk of zealots for a form of government that is hostile to everything for which this country now stands or ever has stood. *I think this fear is groundless.*

There is an amazing concept implicit in the words "I think this fear is groundless": Amazing that the judges of the United States Supreme Court, or any court, would propose to deny freedom of action to the legislative and executive branches of government as they confront the ebbs and flows of the mighty Communist-Socialist tide; amazing that the judicial branch of the government would voluntarily hazard a single element of the security of the Nation on a basis of *winner-take-all.*

-----

[2] On April 26, 1965 it sent two Communist Front cases back to the trial courts because the evidence (some of it dating back several years) was said by the majority of the Court to be "stale."

May 24, 1965 the Supreme Court struck down, 8 to 0, a 1962 statute that authorized the Post Office Department to hold up and destroy unsealed Communist propaganda, unless the addressee requested that it be delivered. November 15, 1965 it ruled that members of the Communist Party need not register under the 1950 Subversive Activities Control Act.

If the winner-take-all prognostication did not have this exalted sponsorship it would not merit discussion, but since the Supreme Court Justices did profess a clear picture of the future, it should be worthwhile to glance outside the legal realm and take note of the fantastic uncertainties inherent in forecasting.

Innumerable specific examples of the unpredictability of the future—of major miscalculations—spring to mind. Among them:

—The wide acceptance as a fact, that the Chinese "Communists" were mere agrarian reformers.

—The prediction of "peace in our time" that was voiced by Prime Minister Chamberlain in 1938.

—The prediction by Hitler that National Socialism would endure a thousand years.

—The belief, attributed to President Roosevelt, that he could outbargain Stalin.

—Notable for the short time between prognostication and refutation was Senator William E. Borah's statement made to Secretary of State Cordell Hull in a conference at the White House on July 18, 1939. In reply to the Secretary's offer to show him telegrams indicating the imminence of war, Borah said that he would not wish to be bound by such information, that he had sources of his own that had sometimes proved more reliable. He said, "My feeling and belief is that we are not going to have a war." Six weeks later World War II commenced when Poland was invaded September 1, 1939. It should be noted that Senator Borah was speaking well within the range of his constitutional and official responsibilities. He was senior minority member of the Foreign Relations Committee of the United States Senate. Evaluation of the prospects for war or peace was part of his job.

Obviously courts are not better equipped for predicting the future than were some of those whose acts were so ill-advised or whose forecasts were so wrong. Nevertheless such forecasting—especially as it reflects un-concern about the potentialities of Marxist enmity—underlies many modern decisions where the issue is subversion versus such rights as freedom of speech.

The most widely known test for limitation of freedom of speech is the one stated by Justice Oliver Wendell Holmes, Jr. in 1919: Does a subversive act present *a clear and present danger?*[3]

The rule is not a wholly satisfactory one, because its application must be subjective. As an example: Consider Fidel Castro when he was just another of a series of leaders of rebellion against the Batista government, head of a band of bearded rebels in the mountains of Oriente province. Would a speech in Havana praising Castro's relatively small force offer a clear and present danger to the powerfully entrenched Batista? Obviously the answer would depend largely on the person questioned, and might have varied from day to day or month to month.

However, Justice Holmes's clear-and-present-danger yardstick undeniably recognized the conflicting problems, and it was quotable. It has been frequently quoted. But generally we have forgotten that Justice Holmes used the

---

[3] *Schenck v. United States,* 249 U S 47 (1919)

phrase in writing a decision *upholding,* not *reversing,* the conviction of a criminal. His 1919 decision offers an excellent gauge of the change in legal thought and action that has occurred in the intervening years.

First, the geopolitical change. In 1919 Russia was the only Bolshevik nation. Now Bolshevik-Communist-Socialism controls impressive fractions of the earth's surface and peoples.

Next, the evolution in decision making:

Justice Holmes (a) in upholding a criminal conviction (b) recognized the possible existence of a danger to our government, although it was then only hull-down on the horizon, and (c) he attempted to establish a standard for adjudication that allowed *a margin of safety* to the government.

Now, in the 1961 cases of Konigsberg and Anastaplo: (a) the issue was the privilege of membership in a learned profession (and possible elevation to a judgeship), not prison versus freedom; (b) danger, of some substantial degree, was in plain view; (c) the opinion offered no yardstick except a Justice's wager on a win-or-lose basis— no margin of safety for the existing government was implicit therein.

If one finds greater wisdom in Justice Holmes's formula than in the modern approach of the judiciary by un-hedged political evaluations, one might be tempted to explain the difference as springing from the Justice's exceptional qualities of mind. But in 1919 his prescience was not unique. Our State Department was even then aware the Bolsheviki were mortal enemies of freedom, and Attorney General A. Mitchell Palmer and (Federal) Bureau of Investigation Director Bruce Bialaski were actively combating subversive activities—to such an extent that their efforts engendered great waves of denunciation and their public careers foundered in the dangerous political seas raised by critics of "red-baiting."

If, as it would appear, Justice Holmes was merely in step with his times in recognizing the right of our government to defend against subversion, may it not be that some of our modern courts are behind the times in their interference with this right of the sovereign?

Our courts should be, although their decisions frequently suggest they are not, cognizant of the fact that every representative government carries in its body cancer cells that can destroy it. Avowed or secretly opposed enemies can seek election or governmental appointment, then from seats of power they can destroy the government whose organization they used as a tool.

In this way Nazism came to power in Germany. The Communist-inspired Popular Front coalition government, a subtle variant of the disease, was almost fatal to a number of governments between World Wars I and II. In Spain, as the government was dying of Popular Front disease, Franco snatched the succession to sovereignty from the expectant Communists. Our State Department urged a Popular Front coalition on a wary Chiang Kai-Shek. The body politic of Czechoslovakia was invaded by the Communist cancer, and died. Italy and France are continually confronted with the Popular Front device. And today it appears in a negotiated guise as the troika government of Laos.

Here in the United States, where we are confident in

the majesty of our 175-year-old Federal Republic, it is easy—far too easy—to assume that no serious threat is posed by the many forces inimical to our way of life. It is pleasant to assume, for example, that no danger impends from an American Communist Party that may have less than a hundred thousand active collaborators and members. However, it should not be an undue imposition on the bench and bar to take stock of the vitality factors of this and other political ideologies—especially since our courts rule so frequently on problems posed by them.

Two novel governmental forms that deify the state appeared dramatically during and after World War I in two dissimilar guises—Fascism and Communism. They are billed as antithetical, but their political structures bear striking similarities; both are based on state socialism, and the action-now propaganda of each has often been known to appeal to the same type of person. The record shows numerous instances in which a former Communist became an ardent Fascist, or vice versa; apparently a mere matter of chance determined by whether an individual was recruited as a member of the highly disciplined Communist Party, or became a fanatical Brown Shirt, Black Shirt, or Falangist.

Although the wave of active Fascist-Socialism in Europe has subsided, Communist-Socialism today is an expanding imperialism; a living, growing, vital force. And this is not surprising for the Communists' techniques, compared with those of the Fascists, show infinitely more subtlety.

Fascist-Socialism—in spite of its strongly nationalistic

tone—had considerable exportability as a political idea. But here again, it is not in the same league with Communist-Socialism. Communist sympathy ranges the world —through party members, fellow travelers, admirers, apologizers-for, do-business-with-ers, novelty lovers, and the gullible who are forever accepting at face value the current phase of Peking or Kremlin policy. Communist Socialism is, in fact, so exportable that it can be rated the most effective colonizing tool yet devised by man.

Its techniques for colonizing are varied. In its efforts to colonize by conquest, Communism has taken the lives of thousands of American boys (54,000 in the Korean War alone; the score is not yet posted for South Vietnam and Latin America) and caused the Nation to spend undreamed of treasure. How then is it possible, nearly a half century after the preliminary blood letting by the Bolskeviki that literate Americans can be oblivious of Communist-Socialism's never-changing evil nature?

But such is the case. Strangely, Communism seems incapable of being recognized by every non-Communist as an undeviatingly cruel and conscienceless bureaucracy. And *the effects of its peculiarly disarming quality is disclosed even in the decisions of our courts.* Some American courts—somehow—manage to remain unconcerned in the face of the record of happenings (as in the following brief dossier) that must be known to every judge in the nation:

In two examples, Poland's soldiery, because of its courage and leadership, was coldly marked by the Soviet for martyrdom.

The first incident was the Communists' mass execution in the Katyn Forest of some 5,000 Polish officers in the

1939 partition of Poland between Russia and Germany.[4] With perfect consistency to the Communist willingness to gain from both sides[5] of any crime, the Soviet Union charged the Nazis with this barbarous act. Later, when the Germans overran the area, international investigators found it had been the U.S.S.R. that murdered the officers. To any thinking person, the purpose of such a massacre is readily apparent: A group of educated and high-principled Poles necessarily included many who undoubtedly would be leaders of opposition to a Communist-Socialist take over of Poland.

The second Polish incident: In 1944, when the Russian army had reached the outskirts of Warsaw, it sent word to the Polish underground that the Soviet troops would launch an attack on the city. They asked the Poles to rise against the Germans in coordination with a scheduled Soviet attack. The Poles were duped into a magnificent revolt against the German forces occupying Warsaw. The Russians rested on their arms across the Vistula River. From August to October, 1944, in 63 days of battle, the Germans killed 250,000 Poles. The Russians did not launch the attack until January, 1945.

----

4 F.J.P. Veale, *War Crimes Discreetly Veiled,* The Devin-Adair Company, New York, 1958. Rebecca West, *The New Meaning of Treason,* Page 301, The Viking Press, 1964. J. K. Zawodny, *Death in The Forest,* also Los Angeles Times, April 18, 1965, Section G.

5 Cuba is suspected of the same tactics in the highly publicized sinking of the Spanish vessel Sierra Aranzazu in September, 1964, according to Robert S. Allen and Paul Scott in their syndicated column of October 20, 1964. The Castro government charged the ship was sunk by Free Cuba raiders, but U. S. Naval Intelligence estimates, based on eyewitness reports, indicate that Castro's raiders sank the vessel.

Again, to the thinking person, the coldly calculated maneuver explains itself. The Russians knew they were winning the war, so they arranged for the Germans to erase most of the Warsaw Poles who were militant, and therefore potentially dangerous to Communist-Socialist rule.

Recounting and analyzing Communist crimes obviously could reach far beyond the space it should occupy here, therefore the following are offered simply as refreshers of memory: The starving of three to five million Russians in 1930-33; the notorious Molotov-Von Ribbentrop deal for concert of action by Communists and Nazis in 1939 and the conquest of Eastern Poland by the U.S.S.R.; the annexation of Estonia, Latvia, and Lithuania with the murder and exile of tens of thousands; Siberian slave labor; the oppression of Jews within Russia; the suppression of religion within Russia; the attack on Finland; the putsch against representative government in Czechoslovakia; the liquidation of over 20 million Chinese;[6] the liquidation of 80,000 to 105,000 Frenchmen, largely by the Communist section of the "partisans" upon the withdrawal of German forces from France;[4] the murder of Mikhailovich by Tito. And the ultimate damning fact—no Communist-Socialist Utopia dares permit emigration!

----

[6] The AFL/CIO's higher estimate of Red murders was cited by William F. Buckley, Jr., (syndicated column 6/4/65) commenting on an ecstatic author's observation about Communist China, that he "found the city to be extremely clean, with almost no flies." Said Buckley, "Absolutely amazing what you can do if you slaughter 25 million people (the figures are the result of researches by the AFL/CIO), enslave 700 million people (the figures are the World Almanac's), and wreck the peace of a continent (the figures are the morticians' of Tibet, Korea, South Vietnam, and Laos)."

Even such a thumbnail listing from the Communist dossier points up to the free world an obvious moral: Every sovereign government—and above all the United States—should spare no pains to keep its powder dry. In this effort every free world government has the right to expect vigilant assistance from its courts of law.

twelve

Sovereignty and Self-Preservation: Where Is the Point of No Return?

Self-preservation is as much the first law of government as it is the first law of nature for every living thing. An existing government may be a noxious weed or the most beautiful plant in the Gardens of History. But, regardless of its quality, its prime function is to survive.

As notable—and highly persuasive—illustrations of the absolute necessity of government looking first to its own survival, consider the governments that were the predecessors of the Nazis and of the Bolsheviks: The Weimar Republic of Germany, The Kerensky Government of Russia. Only in history books do they survive.

Pondering the fate of those two "liberal" sovereigns might be a salutory exercise for contemporary lawyers and

judges because it so happened that Weimar's and Kerensky's failure to stamp out subversive forces loosed the
scourge of Nazi-Socialism and the yet unmeasured evil of
Communist-Socialism upon the world in general—as well
as upon their own citizens.

History, since its beginnings, has recorded little to en-
courage complacency in sovereigns during their periods
of existence. In fact it would scarcely be worth the time
it takes to note even briefly its warnings against that indulgence—if so much modern legal thinking were not the
epitome of complacency.

There is no point where any sovereign's concern about
survival can come to rest. It is a notable historical fact
that regimes are not commonly overthrown when they are
lean and striving, but when they are wealthy and confident.
It is not the hard and ruthless ruler who is deposed, but
the soft and yielding one. It was not the despotic Louis
XIV who lost his head to the guillotine, but the mildly
reform-minded Louis XVI.

Obviously any government protects itself most effectively when it uses the most direct measures to liquidate
those who would overthrow it. Extremes among the available methods are illustrated in the blood purges of Stalin[1]
and Hitler, in the drumhead courtsmartials of Castro, in
the imprisonments in Siberian labor camps, in the calculated reign-of-terror espoused in Lenin's writings *as a
basic strategy*.

Most governments do not use gross terrorist methods,
but every degree that a government withholds its power

---

[1] Khrushchev lacked either the organizational strength or the foresight to emulate the Stalin tactic.

to suppress enemies increases the hazard to its survival. And where a government has achieved enough political maturity to hold periodic, free elections, it is confronted with highly sophisticated problems in guarding its sovereignty.

These problems were clearly recognized at the founding of our Union. And they were taken carefully into account by the drafters of the Constitution when they created a national government with limited powers curtailed by specific restrictions—the right to habeas corpus, bail, trial by jury, prohibition of Bills of Attainder and ex post facto laws. Promptly after the United States of America was established, at its first session, Congress proposed twelve amendments. Ten of these, that came to be known as the Bill of Rights, were adopted by the States as more definite protection for the States and their citizens against the National Government. The political thinking reflected the economic and social background of that time. In those days, property, whether a three-legged stool, a hand-wrought nail, or a bolt of cloth, had been arduously made by the owner or a local artisan, or brought by sailing vessel. Physical dangers attended nearly every activity. Voting was restricted to citizens who were substantial property owners. The voters and the leaders of that period exhibited a genius for the organization of government beyond that shown by any other people at any time in history. Their studied steps to guard the liberty of individuals were carefully balanced against the National Government's essential requirements as a sovereign.

Many of our present day courts of last resort have diverged widely from the Constitution's plan and philosophy. Some, not all, decree ever broader immunities for the criminal and the disloyal; some, not all, make deep incursions into the legislative and executive fields; some, not all, impute to the states the restrictions that were tailored for the limited National Government. Federal Courts, of all levels, assume a right to supersede the work of state courts and to assume the so-called "police power" of the states.

Amazingly, many members of the legal fraternity acquiesce in these trends that are directly opposed to the principles they studied. How can their acquiescence be accounted for?

Some speculation about this phenomenon—even though it be sketchy and inconclusive—should be a worthwhile pursuit for Americans. At the risk of being repetitious, we will venture a short way in such speculation, noting particularly the two differing faces of legal thought and action:

As the reference point never to be disregarded we might note again the one basic and overriding characteristic of human society: Sovereignty is the power of an individual or an organization to impose its will on the inhabitants of a given part of the earth's surface.

Although force may not be conspicuous, it underlies sovereign power. It is against the ever dominant role of force that the actions of today's lawyers and judges must be appraised. And to an alarming extent we observe lawyers espousing causes, and courts issuing decisions that display, in common, an enchanted disregard of known facts about human conduct. They even display minimal regard for the security of the United States. And they do so although confronted with the fact that this is the one nation upon which the geopolitics of the twentieth century has thrust the guardianship of the cause of human freedom.

Many members of the legal fraternity appear to be occupied in placing two different faces on jurisprudence. One face is carved by a large group of public-spirited attorneys. As was suggested in Chapter I, these attorneys among other things are trying to cast the law (via World Peace Through Law) in the grandiose role of 'leading man' on the stage of geopolitics; a role the law is not physically qualified to perform, even if there were an established body of international law.

These men seem not to recognize that sovereignty is based on deeds, not words alone; on power, not principle alone. That Simon Bolivar, Washington, and Garibaldi are remembered as liberators primarily for the reason that they mustered the power to uphold the principles they preached. That they would not be remembered had they failed.

This face is again displayed by many lawyers—speaking persuasively through the House of Delegates of the American Bar Association—recommending that this nation confer on the World Court jurisdiction to try any case against us that the Court would choose to hear. Advice chiefly founded, it seems, on an assumption that the World Court would refrain from assuming jurisdiction over any matter that is of America's *internal* concern. Such a notion shifts the spotlight to another face of modern jurisprudence that has been carved by many decisions of many courts—the lack of judicial self-restraint in our own courts. A most solemn notice of this was made a public record seven years ago by the Chief Justices of the State Supreme Courts:

In 1958 during the American Bar Association convention in Los Angeles, the tenth annual conference of the State Chief Justices addressed an unprecedented petition to the justices of the United States Supreme Court. The drafting Committee's unanimous report was signed by: Frederick W. Brune, Chief Judge of Maryland, Chairman; Albert Conway, Chief Judge of New York; John R. Dethmers, Chief Justice of Michigan; William H. Duckworth, Chief Justice of Georgia; John E. Hickman, Chief Justice of Texas; John E. Martin, Chief Justice of Wisconsin; Martin A. Nelson, Associate Justice of Minnesota; William C. Perry, Chief Justice of Oregon; Taylor H. Stukes, Chief Justice of South Carolina; and Raymond S. Wilkins, Chief Justice of Massachusetts.

The Conference adopted the resolution set forth below by a vote of 36 to 8, with 2 justices absent and 2 abstaining; a voting ratio of 4½ to 1. These high constitutional officers sounded a warning to America and to Americans:

RESOLVED:

1. That this Conference approves the Report of the Committee on Federal-State Relationship as Affected by Judicial Decisions submitted to this meeting.

2. That in the field of federal-state relationships the division of powers between those granted to the national government and those reserved to the state governments should be tested solely by the Constitution of the United States and the Amendments thereto.

3. That this Conference believes that our system of federalism, under which control of matters primarily of national concern is committed to our national government and control of matters primarily of local concern is reserved to the several states, is sound and should be more diligently preserved.

4. That this Conference, while recognizing that the application of constitutional rules to changed condi-

tions must be sufficiently flexible as to make such rules adaptable to altered conditions, believes that a fundamental purpose of having a written constitution is to promote the certainty and stability of the provisions of law set forth in such a constitution.

5. That this Conference hereby respectfully urges that the Supreme Court of the United States, in exercising the great powers confided to it for the determination of questions as to the allocation and extent of national and state powers, respectively, and as to the validity under the Federal Constitution of the exercise of powers reserved to the states, exercise one of the greatest of all judicial powers—the power of judicial self-restraint—by recognizing and giving effect to the difference between that which, on the one hand, the Constitution may prescribe or permit, and that which, on the other, a majority of the Supreme Court, as from time to time constituted, may deem desirable or undesirable, to the end that our system of federalism may continue to function with and through the preservation of local self-government.

That the urging of these high judicial officers went unheeded is demonstrated by many Supreme Court decisions in this volume. And it has also been shown that many state courts are playing self-expanded roles. What does all this portend for America?

At stake today, in the opinion of many citizens, are the priceless fruits of the Constitutional Convention at Philadelphia. True, no respected voices openly denounce Constitutional government, but some acts and attitudes of some members of the legal profession suggest, at best, a masquerade of the American Constitutional plan.

It is obvious there can be no Constitutional government *in fact*, if every specific provision of a constitution is to be overridden by "general welfare," "due process of law," "equal protection of the law" as such terms are freshly interpreted by today's court; or by tomorrow's. There can be no Constitutional government in the American tradition, unless every branch of the government operates exslusively within its sphere and fully respects the spheres of the other two branches; unless the national government is sovereign in its assigned functions, and the states are sovereign in the non-delegated fields, in short, unless the American system of checks and balances can be saved from obliteration.

This Nation was created and came to a glowing maturity under a unique constitutional plan. And its development, too, was unique in that there was thoughtful and jealous adherence to the constitutional form throughout the earlier decades and generations of its existence. Now the most casual observer is conscious of a departure from the text and tradition of the Constitution.

Is there danger to America and to Americans from the trend to abandon true constitutional government? Unquestionably the great underlying principles of America's sovereignty have been attenuated to a point of hazard. Let us not go on to the point of no return.

L'ENVOI
"Good intention will always be pleaded for every assumption of power . . . It is hardly too strong to say that the Constitution was made to guard the people against the dangers of good intentions. There are men in all ages who mean to govern well, but they mean to govern. They promise to be good masters, but they mean to be masters."

DANIEL WEBSTER

APPENDIX A

The following excerpt from a speech made by Governor Franklin D. Roosevelt on March 2, 1930 is reproduced because its authorship will commend the arguments to serious consideration by readers who might otherwise brush them aside.

"As a matter of fact and law, the governing rights of the States are all of those which have not been surrendered to the National Government by the Constitution or its amendments. Wisely or unwisely, people know that under the Eighteenth Amendment Congress has been given the right to legislate on this particular subject [prohibition], but this is not the case in the matter of a great number of other vital problems of government, such as the conduct of *public utilities, of banks, of insurance, of business, of agriculture, of education, of social welfare and of a dozen other important features. In these, Washington must not be encouraged to interfere.*

"The doctrine of regulation and legislation by 'master minds,' in whose judgment and will all the people may gladly and quietly acquiesce, has been too glaringly apparent. . . Were is possible to find 'master minds' so unselfish, so willing to decide unhesitatingly against their own personal interest or private prejudices, men almost godlike in their ability to hold the scales of Justice with an even hand, such a government might be to the interest of the country, but there are none such on our political horizon, and we cannot expect a complete reversal of all the teachings of history.

"Now, to bring about government by oligarchy masquerading as democracy, it is fundamentally essential that practically all authority and control be centralized in our National Government. The individual sovereignty of our States must first be destroyed,* except in mere minor matters of legislation. We are safe from the dangers of any such departure from the principles on which this country was founded just so long as the individual home rule of the States is scrupulously preserved and fought for whenever it seems in danger."

APPENDIX B

The chief service lawyers can render to American civilization is in guiding clients into lawful courses of procedure based on established principles of law. In 1944, when judicial re-making of the law was just becoming a commonplace, Associate Justice Owen J. Roberts tellingly pointed out the value of settled law and the disservice of judicial actions that unsettle the law:

"The evil resulting from overruling earlier considered decisions must be evident. In the present case,[1] the court below naturally felt bound to follow and apply the law as clearly announced by this court. If litigants and lower federal courts are not to do so, the law becomes but a game of chance; instead of settling rights and liabilities it unsettles them. Counsel and parties will bring and prosecute actions in the teeth of the decisions that such actions are not maintainable on the not improbable chance that the asserted rule will be thrown overboard. Defendants will not know whether to litigate or to settle for they will have

---

* Compare with the Hitler dictum at page 39.

[1] *Mahnick v. Southern S. S. Co.* 321 U S 96 (1944)

no assurance that a declared rule will be followed."

Another case[2] in the same year drew this dissent by Justice Roberts:

". . . I have expressed my view with respect to the present policy of the court freely to disregard and to overrule considered decisions and the rules of law announced in them. This tendency, it seems to me, indicates an intolerance for what those who have composed this court in the past have conscientiously and deliberately concluded, and involves an assumption that knowledge and wisdom reside in us which was denied to our predecessors . . .

"The reason for my concern is that the instant decision, overruling that announced about nine years ago, tends to bring adjudications of this tribunal into the same class as a restricted railroad ticket, good for this day and train only. I have no assurance, in view of current decisions, that the opinion announced today may not shortly be repudiated and overruled by justices who deem they have new light on the subject. In the present term the court has overruled three cases.

"In the present case, as in Mahnick v. Southern S. S. Co., the court below relied, as it was bound to, upon our previous decision. As that court points out, the statutes of Texas have not been altered since Grovey v. Townsend was decided. The same resolution is involved as drawn in question in Grovey v. Townsend. Not a fact differentiates that case from this except the names of the parties. . . .

"It is regrettable that in an era marked by doubt and confusion, an era whose greatest need is steadfastness of

---

[2] *Smith v. Allwright,* 321 U S 649 (1944)

thought and purpose, this court, which has been looked to as exhibiting consistency in adjudication, and a steadiness which would hold the balance even in the face of temporary ebbs and flows of opinion, should now itself become the breeder of fresh doubt and confusion in the public mind as to the stability of our institutions."

APPENDIX C

The speech set forth below was delivered by Los Angeles Chief of Police W. H. Parker September 1, 1961, about two months after the decision by the United States Supreme Court of Mapp v. Ohio (page 26). The Chief is a graduate lawyer, which may account for his reasonably objective remarks on a topic that must be highly subjective to any man who is paid by a city to suppress crime. The speech is of interest today because of the ensuing increase of crime.

As the Russian cosmonaut Titov circled the earth each 88.6 minutes in his 10,000 pound vehicle and by means of radio communication transmitted his reactions and observations to his superiors so that all might participate in the realization of this coveted first in space travel, it should have served to humble each of us. It is like standing at the foot of a giant redwood and gazing skyward as we contemplate our individual impact upon mankind and the universe.

None of us could recreate the redwood tree, and few of us possess the intellect and skill required to place a man in orbit and bring him back alive. While each of us is quick to demand our share of the fruits of collective effort, few possess the ability to create the comforts with which we are surrounded. We are unhesitant in our proclaiming individual rights, when they seem to result in subjective benefit, but give little thought to the price society may be paying for our indulgence. We are inclined to look upon the unprecedented materialism with which we are surrounded as a sort of divine birthright to which we are entitled to enduring possession and enjoyment. We give little thought to the efforts, attitudes, and sacrifices of our progenitors who created our luxury in their dedicated quest for the betterment of all mankind. We amplify the recognition of the individual rights imbedded in the concepts of our republic, but tend to ignore any lack of balance with the responsibilities inherent in any self-governing society. It is difficult to reconcile the smugness of our people with the surrounding crises that threaten our very existence.

For more than 34 years, I have devoted my time and energy to the business of policing in the City of the Angels. There were interims such as the year spent at Northwestern University improving academic background in police and traffic administration, and the more than two years in Europe in military government during World War II. It is this combination of experiences that has whetted my consciousness of the peril in which a nation places itself when it becomes careless of its discipline. Man is constantly engaged in an internal conflict as his intellect struggles with his human proclivities for domination of his behavior pattern. When the culture in which he finds himself lacks strong control factors, the basic urges prevail and individual excesses multiply.

Beginning with the cessation of hostilities in World

War II, a progressive revolution against constituted authority has shaken the stability of the entire world. This is a phenomenon which is difficult for me to understand. It resembles a violent reaction to the harsh restrictions imposed upon people in a world at war as the emphasis shifts to uninhibited individual conduct. The police, as the physical symbol of authority, meet the full shock of these assaults. Just last year the London Commissioner of Police informed me that a great many police recruits leave after about two years of service because of the public attitude. While this relationship has rendered it exceedingly difficult to recruit qualified young men into the police service, both here and abroad, there is a deeper significance that could destroy our ability to meet the international challenges both existent and impending.

President Kennedy has made many public statements about the hazards that imperil human freedom and our national survival. I submit that two of these pronouncements are the most profound. First is the statement that we should ask ourselves what we can do for our country rather than what the country can do for us. Later, in commenting on the cold war, he gave one of the answers when he said, "The self-discipline of the free mind must match the iron discipline of the mailed fist."

I doubt that many Americans comprehended the full import of this statement, and yet it may well spell out a condition precedent for our survival. No one doubts that the Soviet bloc constitutes our enemy, and we recognize that the totalitarian rule represented by this group maintains discipline through means of ruthless force or fear. While this type of discipline is repugnant to free men it is possessed of a demonstrated effectiveness. The continuing spread of the iron and bamboo curtains gives mute evidence of this. Technological development under communist direction in potential weapons impresses upon us the seriousness of the threat cultured under the iron discipline of the mailed fist.

If we are to match their level of discipline, how is it to be accomplished? We are a self-governing society. Ours is a government of the people, for the people, and by the people. We do not countenance despotic rule, and we promulgate our own regulations through our elected representatives in the local, state, and national legislative bodies. Our elections are not rigged affairs with a single place for a yes or no vote. Our elections are competitive, and the decision is made by the majority of those who choose to vote. As self-governing people, we possess the ability to control our individual behavior in conformity with the regulations we have thus produced for the security and welfare of our society. These regulations are known as laws, and we all realize it is our solemn obligation to obey these laws—but do we? To the extent we ignore this obligation, we provide a gap between the self-discipline required for our survival and the actual level of our behavior.

How do we measure the level of discipline in this country? There is no existing measure worthy of the name except our crime statistics. With all of the defects in their compilation, they remain the only barometer available. Well, then, what are the trends and how well are we getting along?

Let us glance at recently published statistical reports. The first is called "Crime in the United States" and encompasses the uniform crime reports for the year 1960.

In the summary at the beginning of the report we read: "With 1,861,300 serious offenses reported in 1960, crime continued its upward surge, 14 per cent over 1959. First year of the sixties recorded a new all-time high, with 98 per cent more crime than in 1950. Crime continued to outstrip population growth over 4 to 1. Crime clock shows four serious crimes per minute. Robbery had most significant increase in 1960, up 18 per cent over 1959. Increased police effectiveness resulted in 71 per cent more cases cleared by arrest and 65 per cent more persons charged than in 1950; meanwhile, court convictions up 42 per cent. Arrests totaled 3,640 for every 100,000 persons in 1960. Arrests of persons under 18 more than doubled since 1950, while population of youths, ages 10-17, increased by less than one-half. Forty-eight police employees killed in 1960 and over 9,000 police assaulted."

Let us now look at a report called "Crime in California 1960." Well, there is no encouragement to be found in its pages. Based upon the FBI comparison major crime in California registered a 22.3 per cent increase during 1960 over 1959. The comparable increase for the City of Los Angeles was 18.5 per cent. California enjoys the dubious distinction of having the second highest crime rate in the Nation surpassed only by the State of Nevada. The 1960 rate of Part I offenses (Murder, Rape, Robbery, Burglary, Auto Theft, Felonious Assault, and Theft over $50) per 100,000 population for the five leading states are:

Nevada	1993.1
California	1976.5
Arizona	1638.6
Florida	1609.0
Illinois	1440.4

A shallow and unrealistic reaction to this disturbing increase in criminal incidence would be to criticize the police for failing to stem the tide. The plain unadulterated facts are that the police, individually and collectively, worked more diligently and intelligently last year than ever before. The police are fighting a losing battle by reason of dilution of authority and a social crime product in excess of their repressive ability. Two factors are present in this situation which we cannot afford to ignore. We have no right to expect any increase in the competency or caliber of the police recruits of the future, and local governments cannot afford any substantial increase in policing costs.

One of today's difficulties facing the police administrator is the maintenance of a personnel behavior level in excess of that adhered to by the general population. The moral fiber of those in the police service is bound to compare with that of the general population.

The limited financial income of our municipalities gives little hope of any substantial increase in police expenditures. During this fiscal year, the Police Department alone will cost the City of Los Angeles more than $50,-000,000, while the city struggles to maintain a financial balance. The solution to the problem does not lie in a larger police establishment and more prisons, but in less crime.

Concomitant with the wide-spread assault upon constituted authority has been a general reduction in police authority. These retrenchments have sprung from legislative action and judicial decree with emphasis upon the latter. The disparaging feature of these limitations has been the tendency of their creators to disown any responsibility for the inevitable increase in crime. They have deliberately distorted the effects of their actions by righteously proclaiming that the police can adjust to these restrictions without any debilitation of the public welfare. This was the situation when some of us protested the California adoption of the exclusionary evidence rule in 1955. In the 1960 annual report of the Los Angeles Police Department appears the following statement entitled "A Prophecy Fulfilled": "In April 1955, the Supreme Court of California, in a four to three decision (People v. Cahan) imposed the exclusionary evidence rule upon the courts of this State. Its adoption destroyed over 100 years of precedent. In the minority opinion, the three dissenting justices prophesied, '. . . Thus it appears that the main beneficiaries of the adoption of the exclusionary rule will be those members of the underworld who prey upon law-abiding citizens through their criminal activities. . . .' This prophecy has been fulfilled. Since the decision, crime in the State of California has continued a never-ending upward spiral. Crime in the state has risen 90 per cent since 1954—in the city 72 per cent for the same period!"

The California Supreme Court, in establishing an exclusionary evidence rule of its own, was partially stimulated by the fear that their failure to do so might result in an imposition of the federal rule, thus raising a federal question regarding the seizure of evidence in every criminal case. In fact, in the Cahan decision, the majority opinion stated, "We are not unmindful of the contention that the federal exclusionary rule has been arbitrary in its application and has introduced needless confusion into the law of criminal procedure. . . . In developing a rule of evidence applicable in the state courts, this court is not bound by the decisions that have applied the federal rule, and if it appears that those decisions have developed needless refinements and distinctions, this court need not follow them. Similarly, if the federal cases indicate needless limitations on the right to conduct reasonable searches and seizures or to secure warrants, this court is free to reject them."

The hopes of the California Supreme Court were shattered when on June 19, 1961, the Supreme Court of the United States in the case of Mapp v. Ohio declared the seizure of evidence in criminal cases a question of due process of law applicable to the states by virtue of the 14th Amendment to the U.S. Constitution. Thus, in a further encroachment by the federal government upon state sovereignty, in a field in which there is no federal responsibility, i.e. the enforcement of state and local laws, the Supreme Courts and the legislatures of the fifty states have been deprived of the determination of the rules governing the seizure of evidence in criminal cases. The Mapp case represents another 5 to 4 decision or, as I choose to put it, a majority of one. In the dissent, Mr. Justice Harlan said, "In overruling the Wolf case, the court, in my opinion, has forgotten the sense of judicial restraint which, with due regard to *stare decisis,* is one element that should enter into deciding whether a past decision of this court should be overruled. Apart from that, I also believe that the Wolf rule represents sounder constitutional doctrine than the new rule which now replaces it." I cite this quotation from the dissent in order that you not misjudge the basis of my criticism of the decision. I certainly have no quarrel with the Constitution and the Bill of Rights, and I fully realize that decisions of the Supreme Court based upon their current interpretation of the Constitution must be meticulously obeyed. I am concerned, however, with these changes in the application of the Constitution that serve to increase local costs; deteriorate effective law enforcement on the local level; deprive the states of control over local crime; and, serve to further concentrate authority in the federal government.

The question of the guilt or innocence of the defendant is not involved in the exclusionary evidence rule. It merely provides for a collateral proceeding where a determination of the reasonableness of the search that disclosed the incriminating evidence will determine its admissibility. If the court decides the search was unreasonable, the evidence can be excluded and the guilty criminal freed.

A practical application of this rule is reflected in the recent pirating of airplanes. It was suggested that passengers be searched, but the law permits a search of the person only if the police officer has probable cause for an arrest at the time the search is conducted. Otherwise, weapons discovered concealed on the person searched could not properly be used in evidence against him. Thus, society is in many cases denied the effective application of the experience possessed by the police.

There are two distinct fallacies in the present judicial emphasis upon court supervision of police. The freeing of an obviously guilty criminal in those cases where the *ex post facto* determination of the court brands the evidence proffered by the prosecution as the fruits of an unreasonable search is predicated on the theory that the police must not be allowed to profit by reason of an improper act. This attitude exemplifies the "cops and robbers" contest to which law enforcement has been relegated. It is the guilty criminal who profits when he is given his freedom on a technicality, and it is the innocent victims of his future crimes who lose. The criminal prosecution pits the people of the state, and not the police, in opposition to the criminal. I fail to see how the guilty criminal freed constitutes a personal loss to the police officer who has merely attempted to bring a criminal to justice. The other inconsistency is the failure of the courts to apply the exclusionary rule in civil cases. If the constitutional guarantees are in balance, the litigant in a civil case should be entitled to the same protection from the court on constitutional matters that are afforded the defendant in a criminal action. Yet the defendant in a petty gambling case is entitled to oppose the introduction of the evidence against him on the grounds of unreasonable search or illegal seizure while the defendant in a civil action, who may be a wife and mother fighting for her marriage and the custody of her children, has no right to the exclusion of illegally seized evidence. This double standard is difficult for me to understand.

It appears that society is guilty of a fraud upon itself. Actually, the people do not want all of the laws enforced, but only selectively and sufficiently to maintain a "reasonable" balance. Furthermore, in severely limiting the powers of the police, it is anticipated that the police will ignore these legal limitations when the immediate public welfare appears to demand police lawlessness.

This pragmatic approach to a vital social problem has reaped a bumper crop of crime. This "tongue in cheek" attitude toward criminal depravities has fertilized the criminal field until its nourished depredations threaten to make a mockery of the word "security," and destroy any reasonable protection against criminal attack. We must stop playing these games of deceit and be willing to face the facts with righteous resolution.

The degree to which we have failed in maintaining a balance between crime and punishment is graphically illustrated in two comparative statistics contained in the report on crime in California during 1960. While the rate of increase for the Seven Major Offenses was 19.4 per cent, the rate of increase in superior court filings for these crimes was only 9.7 per cent. This comparison further exemplifies the inability of our present system of criminal justice to keep pace with the rise in crime.

. . . Our international enemies constantly call attention to our publicized lawlessness in belittling Western culture. In East Germany one of the propaganda slogans used to ridicule us reads, "The West are gangsters and racketeers." The propaganda material to support this charge need not be invented. Our films, press stories, periodicals, and published crime statistics give substance to the lie. These factors bear great weight among the undecided of the world as we attempt to attract them to our way of life.

Deeply underlying all of the considerations I have referred to is the question of whether "this Nation or any nation so conceived and so dedicated can long endure." What do the present trends portend for the future? Will America survive as a land of the free, or will it sink into the waves of the sea of oblivion that has engulfed all of man's previous attempts to permanently burst the bonds of servitude?

The real value of history is the ability it gives us to interpret the present and predict the future. What does history tell us concerning the past disposition of nations and cultures that developed the same behavior patterns now present in the United States? In searching for the answer, I suggest we look at an historical treatise written by Oxford historian Charles Reith and called "The Blind Eye of History." In his reasearch, the author traced the police function in all of the nations and civilizations of recorded history. He evaluated the effect of the police function upon the ultimate destiny of these social orders. He has concluded that every nation in history that has failed to enforce its rules has perished. He indicates that the failure to obtain law obedience was an important factor in the decline and fall of these nations. I am certain that the brains in the Kremlin have evaluated history with full and objective vision. It may well be that their hopes for ultimate victory in the cold war are predicated on the self-destruction of our internal order through excesses of which disobedience to law is foremost. If this be true, we must change the trend and my immediate suggestions are elemental:

1. Society must treat crime as it would a contagious disease.
2. Society must stop coddling its criminals.
3. Society must play fair with the police, and provide them with reasonable rules that can be obeyed without destroying police effectiveness.

In closing, let me repeat the words of President Kennedy: "If we are to prevail in the cold war, we must match the iron discipline of the mailed fist with the self-discipline of the free mind."

CASES MENTIONED IN THE TEXT
(ALPHABETICALLY)

INDEX OF TOPICS WITH
CITED CASES AND REFERENCES